WHAT YOU NEED TO KNOW ABOUT DEFENDING YOUR FAITH

12 LESSONS THAT CAN CHANGE YOUR LIFE

MAX ANDERS

AUTHOR OF *30 DAYS TO UNDERSTANDING THE BIBLE*

THOMAS NELSON
Since 1798

NASHVILLE DALLAS MEXICO CITY RIO DE JANEIRO

ISBN: 978-1-4016-7536-3

The library of congress has catalogued the earlier edition of this guide as follows:

Library of Congress Cataloging-in-Publication Data

Anders, Max E., 1947–

    Defending your faith: in 12 lessons/Max Anders.

    p. cm. — (What you need to know about)

    ISBN 0-7852-1192-6

    1. Theology. Doctrinal—Popular works. I. Title. II. Series:

    Anders, Max E., 1947– What you need to know about.

BT77.A463   1998

97-46644

230—dc21

CIP

Printed in the United States of America

12 13 14 15 16 QG 05 04 03 02 01

CONTENTS

INTRODUCTION TO THE
WHAT YOU NEED TO KNOW SERIES

You hold in your hands a tool with enormous potential—the ability to help ground you, and a whole new generation of other Christians, in the basics of the Christian faith.

I believe the times call for just this tool. We face a serious crisis in the church today . . . namely, a generation of Christians who know the truth but do not live it. An even greater challenge is coming straight at us, however: a coming generation of Christians who may not even know the truth!

Many Christian leaders agree that today's evangelical church urgently needs a tool flexible enough to be used by a wide variety of churches to ground current and future generations of Christians in the basics of Scripture and historic Christianity.

This guide, and the whole series from which it comes—the *What You Need to Know* series—can be used by individuals or groups for just that reason.

Here are five other reasons why we believe you will enjoy using this guide:

1. It is easy to read.

You don't want to wade through complicated technical jargon to try to stumble on the important truths you are looking for. This series puts biblical truth right out in the open. It is written in a warm and friendly style, with even a smattering of humor here and there. See if you don't think it is different from anything you have ever read before.

2. It is easy to teach.

You don't have time to spend ten hours preparing for Sunday school, small group, or discipleship lessons. On the other hand, you don't want watered-down material that insults your group's intellect. There is real meat in these pages, but it is presented in a way that is easy to teach. It follows a question-and-answer format that can be used to cover the material, along with discussion questions at the end of each chapter that make it easy to get group interaction going.

3. It is thoroughly biblical.

You believe the Bible and don't want to use anything that isn't thoroughly biblical. This series has been written and reviewed by a team of well-educated, personally committed Christians who have a high view of Scripture, and great care has been taken to reflect what the Bible teaches. If the Bible is unambiguous on a subject, such as the resurrection of Christ, then that subject is presented unambiguously.

4. It respectfully presents differing evangelical positions.

You don't want anyone forcing conclusions on you that you don't agree with. There are many subjects in the Bible on which there is more than one responsible position. When that is the case, this series presents those positions with respect, accuracy, and fairness. In fact, to make sure, a team of evaluators from various evangelical perspectives has reviewed each of the volumes in this series.

5. It lets you follow up with your own convictions and distinctives on a given issue.

You may have convictions on an issue that you want to communicate to the people to whom you are ministering. These books give you that flexibility. After presenting the various responsible positions that may be held on a given subject, you will then find it easy to identify and expand upon your view, or the view of your church.

We send this study guide to you with the prayer that God may use it to help strengthen His church for her work in these days.

HOW TO TEACH THIS BOOK

The books in this series are written so that they can be used as a thirteen-week curriculum, ideal for Sunday school classes or other small group meetings. You will notice that there are only twelve chapters—to allow for a session when you may want to do something else. Every quarter seems to call for at least one different type of session, because of holidays, summer vacation, or other special events. If you use all twelve chapters, and still have a session left in the quarter, have a fellowship meeting with refreshments, and use the time to get to know others better. Or use the session to invite newcomers in hopes they will continue with the course.

All ten books in the series together form a "Basic Knowledge Curriculum" for Christians. Certainly Christians would eventually want to know more than is in these books, but they should not know less. Therefore, the series is excellent for seekers, for new Christians, and for Christians who may not have a solid foundation of biblical education. It is also a good series for those whose biblical education has been spotty.

Of course, the books can also be used in small groups and discipleship groups. If you are studying the book by yourself, you can simply read the chapters and go through the material at the end. If you are using the books to teach others, you might find the following guidelines helpful:

Teaching Outline

1. Begin the session with prayer.

2. Consider having a quiz at the beginning of each meeting over the self-test from the chapter to be studied for that day. The quiz can be optional, or the group may want everyone to commit to it, depending on the setting in which the material is taught. In a small discipleship group or one-on-one, it might be required. In a larger Sunday school class, it might need to be optional.

3. At the beginning of the session, summarize the material. You may want to have class members be prepared to summarize the material. You might want to bring in information that was not covered in the book. There might be some in the class who have not read the material, and this will help catch them up with those who did. Even for those who did read it, a summary will refresh their minds and get everyone into a common mind-set. It may also generate questions and discussion.

4. Discuss the material at the end of the chapters as time permits. Use whatever you think best fits the group.

5. Have a special time for questions and answers, or encourage questions during the course of discussion. If you are asked a question you can't answer (it happens to all of us), just say you don't know, but that you will find out. Then, the following week, you can open the question-and-answer time, or perhaps the discussion time, with the answer to the question from last week.

6. Close with prayer.

You may have other things you would like to incorporate, and flexibility is the key to success. These suggestions are given only to guide, not to dictate. Prayerfully choose a plan suited to your circumstances.

CHAPTER 1

WHAT IS TRUTH?

Truth is incontrovertible. Panic may resent it; ignorance may deride it; malice may distort it; but there it is.
—**Sir Winston Churchill**

G ary Paulsen was running the Iditerod dogsled race from Anchorage to Nome, Alaska, for the first time. He edged his dogs onto the ice where they ran easily for hours. Then suddenly everything changed:

> In the first instant I saw Cookie alter her pace . . . almost a walk, and her tail shot up to the question-mark position. If she was confident about things it hung straight down and to the rear, and the height it went up was in direct proportion to what she perceived as risk. I was very much in tune with the position of her tail—lived by it—and now it was straight up, the tip curved over in a question mark. At the same time she "got light." I felt my heart freeze. When she went up on her tiptoes and tried to be lighter it meant only one thing—bad ice.
>
> Half a second later I felt the sled move. It was the same movement an earthquake makes.

Paulsen goes on to say:

> Initially there had been no visual indication of the ice changing. I assumed it was six or eight feet thick—it had density. But . . . it was new ice, very new, with a dusting of snow blown over it. It wasn't a foot thick, perhaps only two inches, and it was . . . heaving with underwater surges.
>
> I grabbed the catch rope and fell back from the sled on my stomach, my legs open to spread the weight. At the same time I yelled:
>
> "Gee around!"
>
> It was an old trapline command and wouldn't work on the race dogs. But Cookie knew it meant to swing out to the right and bring the team back around to get out of a tight spot.

They fought her for a bit, tried to go straight, but she found a crack in the surface and got her nails in and dragged them around with me skidding in back on my stomach.

We went that way for a hundred yards or so when I saw Cookie's tail drop and she headed out almost straight east. I felt a bump as my stomach slid off the bad ice and onto the older ice pan.

Had Paulsen hit the bad ice an hour sooner, he would have gone through the ice. He said, "People die every year on the ice." Some native women have been widowed several times by the time they are twenty-five, husbands lost on sea ice (*Winterdance*, 243–245).

IN THIS CHAPTER WE LEARN THAT . . .

1. The contemporary crisis concerns whether or not objective truth exists and how well people can know it.

2. The Bible views truth as objective, coming from God Himself, and something that can be known, as fully as God permits.

3. We combine a credible lifestyle with an appropriate presentation of truth.

4. Many people deny the existence of truth and ignore the gospel because they do not want to be accountable to it.

It is a dangerous thing when part of the whole breaks off and starts floating away. It means almost certain calamity to those floating away. In a sense, that is what is happening in Western society today. Most Westerners (including Europeans and North Americans and those influenced by American and European ways of thinking) used to share a lot of common ground about the nature of truth, on moral, spiritual, political, and scientific issues. Today there is a crisis over whether truth can be known at all.

WHAT IS THE CONTEMPORARY CRISIS OVER TRUTH?

*The contemporary crisis concerns whether or not objective
truth exists and how well people can know it.*

Chuck Colson has written that the confusion over truth is the fundamental crisis of our age.

> What good does it do to tell people, "The Bible says . . . ," if two-thirds of our listeners don't believe the Bible is true? What good does it do for us to say Jesus is the truth if two-thirds of the American people believe there is no such thing as truth? This is not to deny that the Word of God has the power to convince even the hardest heart. But if Christians are to be heard by the modern mind and make effective inroads into our culture, we must first develop what Francis Schaeffer called a cultural apologetic: We must defend the very concept of truth. (Introduction to *Can Man Live Without God?* by Ravi Zacharias, ix–x)

The loss of confidence in truth can be illustrated from a number of areas of knowledge.

The Loss of Confidence in Truth in Morality

First, people have become uncertain about what's right and wrong, what's moral and what's immoral. Alasdair MacIntyre has argued in his book *A Short History of Ethics* that the loss of strong moral beliefs can be traced back to the Enlightenment, and, in particular, to the views of the philosopher Immanuel Kant (1724–1804).

The Enlightenment refers to a time when European philosophers like Kant, Voltaire, and David Hume believed that there was a new way to determine truth and goodness, apart from the authority of the church or the Bible. While the Enlightenment philosophers were basically skeptical about Christianity, they were very certain about their own "rational" solutions to moral and intellectual problems. MacIntyre said that since the time of Kant and the Enlightenment, "'the acids of individualism' have eaten at the social unity that used to exist on matters of good and bad." What used to be the solid piece of ice—nearly universal agreement on what was wrong and right—cracked into fragmented pieces. Now people in our society disagree considerably about what is right and wrong.

Social unity has been eroded.

11

This breakdown in moral values can be seen all around us. For example, morality is viewed as simply a product of culture. What is right in America is not necessarily right in Saudi Arabia. And who are "we" to tell others how to live? This kind of view is represented in the astonishing fact that, as John Leo reported in the July 27, 1997, edition of *U.S. News & World Report*, some American college students won't condemn Hitler for the Holocaust. "After all, from the Nazi point of view, Hitler believed he was doing the right thing."

The clash over right and wrong plays itself out daily on television talk shows. Every day guests defend practices and beliefs that would only be discussed privately—and then only rarely—forty years ago. Everything is defended by statements like: "Who are you to tell me what is right?" or "I am happy in what I am doing, and it is not hurting anybody, so why does it matter to you?"

The Loss of Confidence in Truth in Religion

People have also lost confidence in religious beliefs. If you and I could travel back to the year 1250 and sit in a class at the University of Paris, we would probably notice that everybody basically shared the same views. There was really only one church in Western Europe, and nobody was in a mood to question the pope.

Three centuries later, a young German monk protested some of the errors of the pope of Rome. Luther said: "My conscience is bound by the word of God. Here I stand! I can do no other." Those of us who are Protestants look to Luther as our hero. We love his courage to stand for Bible-based truth. Luther was confident in his religion, and so was John Calvin, another great reformer.

A skeptical mind-set has been unleashed.

There was an unintended negative spin to what Luther and Calvin did, however. Since they questioned the pope, who was believed to speak with the full authority of Christ, they opened the door to having their own beliefs questioned by others. This unleashed an overall critical, even skeptical, mind-set. This mind-set in Protestant churches has encouraged hundreds of churches to split from parent churches, until today when we have scores of denominations in America. The unity in the church that Jesus prayed for has not been realized.

Of course, the Protestant-Catholic split and the creation of all sorts of Protestant churches is not the end of the story. In the nineteenth century there was an emergence of radically new religious traditions (cults) in America. Joseph Smith started the Mormon church. Mary Baker Eddy introduced us to Christian Science.

Madame Blavatsky started Theosophy, a precursor to the New Age Movement. And the list goes on. No wonder there is a loss of confidence in religion.

The Loss of Confidence in Truth Itself

Confusion about moral and spiritual truth has led to bewilderment about the very notion of truth itself. Many professors in Western universities have argued that truth is subjective and can only be understood through the perspective of our personal experience, that it is a culturally created reality like our views of morality. What is true for one group is not necessarily true for another. In fact, they believe, truth is a very individual thing, if there is even such a thing as truth.

This perspective concerning truth is often called postmodernism. This relative, subjective, and skeptical view of truth is a reaction against earlier "modern" understandings of reason and truth. Basically, Enlightenment philosophers replaced religion with reason and were as dogmatic about their trust in reason as Christians had been about their trust in divine revelation. Modernism, the child of the Enlightenment, has been confident that truth exists and that it is the same for all people. It was sure that reason, aided by the modern scientific method of observation and experimentation, enables us to discover truth. The postmodern mind, however, lacks confidence both in Christian religion and in the views of the modern philosopher or scientist. Postmodernists like Jacques Derrida (derry-dah) are skeptical about every philosophy or ideology or religion, though, of course, he tends to like postmodernism!

> **Postmodernists insist on tolerance.**

Postmodernism is partly born out of a recognition of the diverse moral and spiritual views in the marketplace of ideas. This is not the whole story, however. Postmodernists have also seen how the "truth" or "science" can be used to sanction evil. Think of the justification of the slave trade by Christians in the nineteenth century in America. Nazi ideology was advocated by brilliant philosophers, scientists, and theologians and Bible scholars. Postmodernists like Derrida or Michel Foucault (fu-koh) have seen how intellectuals can defend any position or theory, depending on who is paying or who has the social or political power.

Tolerance is perhaps the most important virtue to postmodern society, and intolerance the most serious vice. Of course, postmodernism can celebrate Christianity if it is viewed as simply another path of spirituality. So one can hear this kind of praise: "Oh, that's wonderful that you are a Christian. It is great that you have found meaning in following Jesus. I, too, have found meaning. I have rediscovered my past life as a Native American shaman [medicine man] and am now into tribal chanting as my mystical path. It is so spiritual. I feel so close to God and nature when I do it. Isn't that wonderful? We're both spiritual!"

HOW DOES THE BIBLE VIEW TRUTH?

The Bible views truth as objective, coming from God Himself, and
something that can be known, as fully as God permits.

The Bible teaches that truth exists and can be known. We can share postmodernism's distrust of Enlightenment rationalism and postmodernism's doubt that modern science operates with total objectivity. With postmodernists, we agree that the personal will of philosophers and scientists shapes how they think and what conclusions they reach. We all tend to see what we want to and even to force what we see into our own agendas, to justify what we want the truth to be. Yet as Christians, we believe that God has revealed truth through His prophets, apostles, and Son, and that this truth is preserved for us in inspired Scripture. So we do not share the postmodern anxiety about truth.

The Bible emphasizes that truth comes from within God Himself. In the Gospel of John, Jesus said, "I am . . . the truth," not *a* truth (14:6). Jesus spoke of truth in these ways too:

- "You shall know the truth, and the truth shall make you free" (John 8:32).
- "When He, the Spirit of truth, has come, He will guide you into all truth" (John 16:13).
- "Sanctify them by Your truth. Your word is truth" (John 17:17).

The apostle Paul was equally unambiguous:

- "The truth is in Jesus" (Ephesians 4:21).
- "For this is good and acceptable in the sight of God our Savior, who desires all men to be saved and to come to the knowledge of the truth" (1 Timothy 2:3–4).

To agree with the Bible that truth is objective (existing whether or not we know or accept it), absolute (unchanging), and universal (true for everyone) is not to say that we know truth completely and purely. We must admit that we do not have a perfect grasp of the truth that God has given us. Godly, well-informed, and intelligent Christians disagree over many things in the Bible—such as the sovereignty of God and the free will of man, or Bible prophecy, or how we should baptize. Therefore, we should not overstate our case when discussing truth. We may believe something to be true (such as how to baptize) without being able to prove to someone else that it is true.

As Francis Schaeffer used to say, we must be careful to say all that Scripture says, and we must be equally careful not to say more than Scripture says. As 1 Corinthians 13:9–13 teaches, it is not until we stand before Jesus that we will know and understand truth perfectly. When presenting truth, we should have a certain humility that acknowledges our imperfect grasp of truth, and that treats others with respect even if we do not agree with them.

> **Moral truth is binding on everyone.**

Nevertheless, we do not determine our own truth, as postmodernists claim. Instead, we accept and practice the truth as it is revealed in Jesus, who is the truth. And in areas outside God's special revelation through Jesus and the Scriptures, we reject as false any claims to truth that are not in harmony with what we understand of revealed truth.

HOW CAN WE PRESENT AND DEFEND THE TRUTH EFFECTIVELY?

We combine a credible lifestyle with an appropriate presentation of truth.

While we believe that truth is absolute, there are three important ways we may grasp truth: by reason, by faith, and by experience.

1. Knowing Truth Through Reason

Many Christians are influenced by fact-based knowledge and careful reasoning based on that knowledge. It is important to them that their faith be rooted in facts and that it be reasonable. Christian apologetics, the study and practice of defending our faith, has been influenced heavily by rationalism, the belief that truth is grasped by reason, even though Christians believe that God is the ultimate source of truth. This means that Christian apologetics can use reason, but it should not be limited only to what the human mind can understand. Thomas Aquinas was shaped significantly by the rationalism of Aristotle, and so he offered us five proofs for God's existence. Josh McDowell, a well-known contemporary evangelical philosopher, loves to present very careful reasons and historical evidences in defense of Christian beliefs.

2. Knowing Truth Through Faith

Other Christians, on the other hand, have been influenced by an outlook known as fideism (fee-day-ism). This view is prominent in Reformed or Calvinistic theology and in some Catholic writers. It says that we find truth by first trusting in God and then following His revelation as the accurate map of all reality. This quote from C. S. Lewis expresses the fideist's perspective (although Lewis himself did not rely only on fideism in his defense of the faith): "I believe in Christianity as I believe in the sun—not only because I see it, but because *by it I see everything else*" (emphasis mine). Human reason is fallible and gives no ultimate certainty. Faith rests in God who alone is the anchor of truth.

Cornelius Van Til, a famous Christian apologist, advanced a version of fideism in contending that one's presuppositions determine everything. Van Til, who taught for forty years at Westminster Theological Seminary, believed that unless one presupposes that God has given truth, there is no way for humans to be certain of anything. For Van Til, only the assumption that God is sovereign and has revealed the truth in the Bible will save humanity from the otherwise confusing voices of human reason. From the Lewis quote, Van Til would emphasize that only by the light of God's revelation—and not by human reason—could he truly see or understand anything else.

> **Fideism trusts God to reveal truth.**

3. Knowing Truth Through Experience

Still other Christians emphasize experience in defending their faith. They might refer to their conversion experience as proof for their faith, or talk about a mystical moment in their lives, or describe an answer to prayer, or share an example of divine healing. Still others might talk about a time when they believe God gave them precise, accurate knowledge about a future event or about another person's need as evidence that God is real. Or they may rely on a deep sense of intuition that the gospel has what J. B. Phillips called "the ring of truth" to it.

I remember an example of this in my own life. Shortly after becoming a Christian, I began to have doubts. One day, however, as I was reading 2 Corinthians 5:17, the passage jumped out at me: "Therefore, if anyone is in Christ, he is a new creation; old things have passed away; behold, all things have become new." I realized that I had stopped swearing, stopped smoking, stopped drinking, and stopped being so preoccupied with girls—things I had tried unsuccessfully to stop doing before my conversion. This experience persuaded me that I had, indeed, become a Christian.

Keeping Truth in Balance

As we look at each of these three avenues for perceiving truth, we can see value in each of them. At times, fact-based information is important to us, while at other times faith provides the light by which we can see the truth, and at still other times, our experience validates truth to us. So it is with those to whom we share our faith. Sometimes we may emphasize facts and reasoning to others, while at other times, we may insist that only by seeing reality by the light that God's revelation provides will it make much sense. At still other times, our personal testimony to meeting and knowing the Lord may be the most effective presentation or response. Because the people we will talk with and the situations in which we will meet them differ so much, we will probably find some combination of these three ways to be most effective.

Along with presenting biblical truth in an appropriate way, we must personally live out a biblical lifestyle. Whether one is dealing with a modern or postmodern person, the openness to a religious position depends on truth claims being wedded with an attractive lifestyle. People are more turned off by a person they can't handle than a doctrine they can't swallow. For example, everyone I have spoken to who has converted, or considered converting, to Mormonism as an adult did so not because of the compelling doctrine but because of the compelling lives of the Mormons they know. This should be a clue to how we reach out to the modern and the postmodern mind.

We can learn from postmodernism's concern about fairness and the rights of the defenseless. Christians certainly can agree that in the areas of race, gender, and handicaps, we must "do unto others as we would have others do unto us." If we would not like to be discriminated against, we must not discriminate. We must try to protect those who cannot protect themselves.

WHY I NEED TO KNOW THIS

I need to know this so that I do not fall into the trap of accepting an unbiblical view of truth. I need to stand firm on the central claims of the gospel as truth, and I need to help others stand on this same reality, since the battle for truth is one of the most important battles of our day. Yet I need to know how others think about truth so that I can talk with them effectively.

I also need to realize that knowing truth is not enough. It must be presented to others from the foundation of a winsome lifestyle, taking others' perceptions into account as I present truth to them.

We can also learn from the postmodernist's passion for ecological issues. It is a matter of God-appointed stewardship that we are to take care of the earth on which we live and depend. Industrial civilization has fouled the nest we live in, and we all are paying a tremendous price as a result. We cannot violate the earth, air, and water without violating ourselves. While we have different reasons than postmodernists for wanting to nurture the environment back to health, the goal is the same.

Postmodernists value relationships.

Building on these areas of common ground, the Christian can begin to talk with postmodernists about what we agree on, and then move on to other areas as we can. No matter what the outcome of our witness to or defense of our faith, we must be people of depth, sensitivity, and compassion who live what we say and who live in community with other believers. The human heart with which we share the gospel of Christ never loses its need for the fundamental combination of truth, love, and community.

WHY DO PEOPLE DENY THE EXISTENCE OF TRUTH?

Many people deny the existence of truth and ignore the gospel because they do not want to be accountable to it.

Where does the contemporary denial of truth come from? How has it come to be so prevalent? What accounts for this historic and ominous shift in thinking? Many people today have this mind-set because they have been indoctrinated and deceived by those who have taught them. They are, perhaps, innocent "believers." Others hold to this mind-set because they want to. It fits their personal agenda, and if so, there are none so blind as those who will not see.

A number of years ago, I witnessed a striking example of how one's desire to see can affect the ability to see. It provided a remarkable example of humanity's willingness, on occasion, to dodge the truth, no matter how obvious it is. I was young enough that I still lived at home with my parents, and my older sister, Mary (name changed to protect my sister), and her husband and their little boy were visiting our home. My three-year-old nephew, Don (name changed to protect me; he's much bigger than I am now!), had been playing with some toys. It was time to leave, so my sister said, "Don, pick up those toys and put them away so we can go home."

Desire affects one's perception of truth.

To fully understand what happened next, it is important to understand that the toys were in the middle of the living room floor in full view of everyone in the room.

Don looked at Mary and in his cutest little three-year-old voice said, "What toys?"

Mary, assuming a careless oversight on his part, patiently replied, "Those toys over there," and pointed to them.

Don deliberately looked in a slightly different direction and asked, "Where?"

Mary cast a puzzled glance at him and said, "Over there," and pointed a little more obviously.

But Don overcorrected. He turned too far in the other direction and stared at a perfectly bare floor. "Where?" he asked, as innocently as a fox in a hen house. He was playing his mother like a master plays a violin.

> We must be willing to go where truth leads.

Mary could not quite believe what she was witnessing. She began to get exasperated as she made it plain to him exactly what direction to look for the toys in question.

In a final virtuoso move, Don turned and looked behind him, nearly the opposite direction of Mary's frantic gesticulations. "Where?" he wheedled, with the purity of a saint.

This last refusal to see the obvious was more than Mary's nerves could withstand. She got up, walked over to Don, held his head in her hands, guided him over to the toys, and tilted his head down. He finally saw them. "There," she said. "Pick them up!"

I was astonished at Don's doomed approach to the problem. I couldn't believe the audacity that was possible from a three-year-old. How long did he think he could string this out?

The problem wasn't that Don couldn't see the toys. It was that he refused to see them. His eyesight was perfectly adequate, but as long as he could pretend not to see them, he could avoid the responsibility of picking them up. He could not be held accountable to pick up something he could not see.

I have often thought that this is similar to knowing God. In many cases, I do not believe the problem is that people cannot know or believe in God, but that they do not want to. Like Don, they conduct command performances with virtuoso skill, exhibiting profoundly creative ways of refusing to see the obvious.

In order to discover truth about God, one has to be willing to go where the truth takes him. Truth, then, demands a response. If one is not willing to go where the evidence leads, he is liable never to find God. And at the bottom of his soul, perhaps he doesn't want to.

It is like the person who has cancer but doesn't know it or, more important, doesn't want to face it. He exhibits some suspicious symptoms that make him wonder, but he often lives in denial, simply putting the possibility of cancer out of his mind. Some people who have this mind-set never go to the doctor until the symptoms become so bad they must go. And then it is too late. Similarly, people can be in denial about the possibility of a God because they don't want to face the consequences; they put Him out of their minds until it is too late.

Aldous Huxley is a good example of someone who accepted a non-Christian view of life and willingly embraced the meaninglessness connected to his religious views. He stated why clearly in his own words:

> For myself, as, no doubt, for most of my contemporaries, the philosophy of meaninglessness was essentially an instrument of liberation. . . . We objected to . . . morality because it interfered with our sexual freedom.

Huxley stated frankly that he decided not to believe in God because believing in God limited his sexual freedom; not believing in God gave him all the sexual freedom he wanted. Huxley wrote:

> I had motives for not wanting the world to have meaning; consequently I assumed that it had none, and was able without any difficulty to find satisfying reasons for this assumption. Most ignorance is vincible (able to be overcome) ignorance. We don't know because we don't want to know. It is our will that decides how and upon what subjects we shall use our intelligence. Those who detect no meaning in the world generally do so because, for one reason or another, it suits their [desires] that the world should be meaningless. (*Ends and Means*, 273)

That many choose to ignore evidence that truth exists and that the gospel is true only confirms what 2 Peter 3:3–5 says:

> First of all, you must understand that in the last days scoffers will come, scoffing and following their own evil desires. They will say, "Where is this 'coming' he promised? Ever since our fathers died, everything goes on as it has since the beginning of creation." But they deliberately forget. (NIV)

They deliberately forgot what they knew about creation and about the coming of the Lord. Peter said they deliberately forgot the truth.

The apostle Paul supported the same idea in Romans 1:18–21:

> For the wrath of God is revealed from heaven against all ungodliness and unrigh-
> teousness of men, who suppress the truth in unrighteousness, because what may
> be known of God is manifest in them, for God has shown it to them. For since the
> creation of the world His invisible attributes are clearly seen, being understood
> by the things that are made, even His eternal power and Godhead, so that they
> are without excuse, because, although they knew God, they did not glorify Him
> as God, nor were thankful, but became futile in their thoughts, and their foolish
> hearts were darkened.

Paul reported that people suppress the truth, and in doing so their thoughts
become futile and their hearts become darkened. When one reads the works of
some atheists and other non-Christian writers who suppress the truth, one sees
how the futility and darkness of their minds has produced answers that are patently
empty and tragic or mind-numbing in complexity and confusion. But, if one will
not believe the truth, he must accept the lie, no matter how complicated or unreasonable or uncomfortable it may be.

CONCLUSION

Obviously, Christian confidence about truth will not automatically lead people to
Christ. Jesus said, "No one can come to Me unless the Father who sent Me draws
him" (John 6:44). Ultimately, whether or not people acknowledge and respond to
truth is a matter between them and God. Nor will the defense of Christian truth
claims necessarily win acceptance. However, we are commanded in Scripture to
defend our faith. Surely it helps to understand key points in this chapter:

1. The contemporary crisis in truth stems from the arrogance and domination of
   others that went along with much of the Enlightenment and modern certainty
   about truth. The Christian certainty of truth is different from Enlightenment
   certainty. Christian certainty comes from confidence in God's revelation of
   truth and must be joined with humility. Believers in truth must be humble
   because they do not know truth completely or purely and because they do
   not own or control the truth, but are called instead to submit to and obey the
   truth—as it is revealed in Jesus.

2. Postmodernism rightly rejects the modern abuses of the notion of objective,
   absolute, and universal truth. Postmodernism also rightly acknowledges that
   our desires—what we would like the truth to be—exert a strong force on what

we finally say is the truth. To this point, the biblical view of truth agrees. But postmodernism makes a major distinction in saying there is no truly, absolute truth. God exists and He has revealed truth. His existence and His truth are not destroyed by our ignorance, indifference, or outright rejection—but we are. And His revelation of truth is the basis for our finding any and all truth. To deny truth itself is, finally, to deny God.

3. It must be noted that many believers today consider themselves to be postmodern. It is, therefore, important for all Christians to be faithful to the truth—to understand, present, and defend it as best we can. We can do no less as we follow the One who said: "I am the way, the truth, and the life."

SPEED BUMP!

Slow down to be sure you've gotten the main points from this chapter.

Q1. What is the contemporary crisis over truth?

A1. The contemporary crisis concerns whether or not *objective truth* exists and how well people can know it.

Q2. How does the Bible view truth?

A2. The Bible views truth as *objective*, coming from God Himself, and something that can be known, as fully as God permits.

Q3. How can we present and defend the truth effectively?

A3. We combine a credible *lifestyle* with an appropriate presentation of truth.

Q4. Why do people deny the existence of truth?

A4. Many people deny the existence of truth and ignore the gospel because they do not want to be *accountable* to it.

FILL IN THE BLANK

Q1. What is the contemporary crisis over truth?

A1. The contemporary crisis concerns whether or not _____ _____ exists and how well people can know it.

Q2. How does the Bible view truth?

A2. The Bible views truth as _____, coming from God Himself, and something that can be known, as fully as God permits.

Q3. How can we present and defend the truth effectively?

A3. We combine a credible _____ with an appropriate presentation of truth.

Q4. Why do people deny the existence of truth?

A4. Many people deny the existence of truth and ignore the gospel because they do not want to be _____ to it.

FOR FURTHER THOUGHT AND DISCUSSION

1. How has your perception of truth changed as a result of studying this chapter?

2. Do you understand or have any appreciation for postmodernism?

3. What approach or approaches to defending your faith do you like the most? What can you do to be a more effective champion of truth?

WHAT IF I DON'T BELIEVE?

If I don't believe that truth is clear since it is rooted in the certain promises of God in Jesus, I am cast adrift on a sea of uncertainty to make my way through this life by trial and error as best I can, and my future beyond death is equally uncertain.

FOR FURTHER STUDY

1. Scripture

- John 8:32
- John 16:13
- John 17:17
- Ephesians 4:21
- 1 Timothy 2:3–4

2. Books

Can Man Live Without God? Ravi Zacharias
A Primer on Postmodernism, Stanley J. Grenz
The Universe Next Door, James Sire
The Death of Truth, Dennis McCallum (Ed.)

CHAPTER 2

WHY DO WE BELIEVE THAT GOD EXISTS?

I can see how it might be possible for a man to look down upon the earth and be an atheist, but I cannot conceive how he could look up into the heavens and say there is no God.
—**Abraham Lincoln**

In what was billed as the "trial of the century," celebrated football Hall-of-Famer, movie star, and television personality O. J. Simpson was accused of murdering his former wife Nicole Brown and the man he thought was her lover. The criminal trial dominated the news and the television talk shows. Books were written about it before it was even over. Eventually, O. J. was acquitted.

The notable thing to me, however, was the fact that people had their minds made up concerning his guilt before the trial ever started. In a startling lapse of concern for judicial process, news commentators asked people before the evidence was presented whether they thought O. J. was guilty. To a striking degree, the black population thought he was innocent, and the white population thought he was guilty.

The final verdict did little to change people's opinions. With a few individual exceptions, the people who thought he was guilty before the trial thought he was guilty after the trial, and vice versa. The evidence presented at the trial seemed almost beside the point. A lot of people apparently interpreted the evidence pretty much the way they wanted to.

I will never forget my outrage and incredulity at people voicing their opinions before the evidence was presented. How could they have an opinion? They didn't know yet what had happened. Opinion followed prejudice.

The same thing happens when people make a decision about God. They often have an opinion about God that is formed at an early age, and tend to interpret the evidence according to their prejudice. In this chapter, we want to look at reasons to believe in God, but in doing so we will also investigate the role of prejudice.

IN THIS CHAPTER WE LEARN THAT . . .

1. Some people reject God because the world is inconsistent with their concept of God.

2. People accept God because the existence of God is the best explanation for the world as it is.

3. We often believe what we want to believe regardless of the evidence.

People hold many different ideas about who God is. Some think He is a compassionate being who only rewards and never punishes. Others think God is an impersonal force that exerts influence on the universe according to certain laws and principles. Still others believe that God is in everything, and everything is God. This book will investigate the claims of the Bible regarding who God is.

WHY WOULD SOMEONE NOT BELIEVE IN GOD?

Some people reject God because the world is inconsistent with their concept of God.

There are many people today, especially in the scientific and educational communities—the intellectual elite of our nation—who do not believe in God. There are several common reasons why.

1. Scientific Evidence

Some believe that, because of what we have learned about the world through scientific discoveries, it is unintellectual to believe in God. Now that we have the theory of evolution, they suggest, and can explain the origin and development of the universe without leaning on the "crutch" of religion, we can see how primitive and superstitious it is to think that God created the world. Evolution is now established in these circles as the world view of choice by an apparent majority of scientists and educators. It has become so pervasive that, except for those who have embraced a creationist worldview, no other possibility is even considered.

The issue is not some supposed conflict between the God of the Bible and scientific information. The theory of evolution is far from being proved, however. In fact, the more information we gain about the world on the very small level of individual cells, DNA, and biochemistry of the human body, the more complex we realize it is, and the less and less likely it is that evolution can account for the level of complexity we see in creation.

All scientific inquiry is based on the assumption that there is order in the physical world. Why should there be order if the world came about by random chance? The physical laws and chemical makeup of living things cannot explain human personality, human behavior and reason, human longing, religion, or morality. There is no scientific information that has been found or will be found that will lay to rest the God of the Bible. This anvil breaks all hammers.

God and science are not in conflict.

2. Suffering

A second reason many people reject the God of the Bible today is because of human suffering. As we look at the flood of information from around the globe that brings the reality of human suffering right into our dinner-hour living rooms, we must be deeply touched or callused. Global suffering has always been a reality, but we have not always been witness to it. It used to be that floods drowned thousands in India, but we never knew it. Now, we watch the bodies float downstream on the evening news. There are those who watch such images and ask, "How can a good God allow such suffering?"

3. Religious Pluralism

To the modern mind, it seems unfair for the God of the Bible to deny salvation to those who sincerely worship another god. It doesn't matter what you believe, they think, as long as you are sincere. When the Bible says that God will condemn those who have not worshiped Him, many people reject the God of the Bible. How can it be fair for someone to be condemned for not believing in God if they haven't even heard of Him? "If that is your God," they reason, "I don't want any part of Him."

To avoid this view of such a narrow-minded and unfair God, many people believe that God will overlook the ignorance of those who worship other gods. "All roads at the base of the mountain lead to the same top," they reason.

WHY WOULD SOMEONE BELIEVE IN GOD?

People accept God because the existence of God is the best explanation for the world as it is.

Although the reasons for not believing in God include some valid concerns, they are not the whole picture. Many of the reasons advanced for believing in God also address those problems that have been raised. If someone were to approach the world with as open a mind as possible, he would find powerful evidence to support the possibility of God's existence. In fact, philosophers have, for centuries, acknowledged the existence of natural evidence for God's existence.

1. The Existence of the World

Jean-Paul Sarte, a French philosopher, once said, "The greatest philosophical question is, 'Why is there something rather than nothing?'" I think he is right. Anything we believe must have an answer to that question, and a belief in God gives a credible explanation for that question.

Since there is something, we must either say that (1) the "something" is eternal, and it has always existed, or (2) originally there was "nothing" and something has come from nothing, or (3) someone created the "something."

Only in the last 150 years or so have civilizations believed anything except that the universe was created by supernatural power. However, with the theory of evolution, people were given an explanation for the universe that didn't require a God. But even evolutionists have a difficult time explaining where the universe came from. They have two choices: one, that God created the universe; or, two, that the universe came into existence by itself. If you believe the latter, you must also believe that the universe came from nothing, or that the stuff the universe came from has always existed. Both of those options are difficult for me to swallow.

A prevailing scientific viewpoint is that matter is eternal—it has always been here. And after an interminable length of time, this matter simmered and cooked and boiled, and finally exploded in one great big bang. All the matter began flying out to the far corners of the universe and, as it cooled, it formed the stars and planets as we see them today.

It all begins with God.

Then on our own planet, things simmered and cooked and boiled and pretty soon life began in some primitive form. Then it grew and began throwing off shoots. Some became plant and some became animal. Of the animals, some became mice and some became monkeys and some became men. It's all random chance, scientists say—all one great big happy accident. But there are several lethal flaws with that explanation.

First, science doesn't support it adequately. If you believe the big bang theory together with evolution, then, as Francis Schaeffer, an evangelical scholar of the last generation used to say, you are locked into the equation "Nothing + The Impersonal + Time + Chance = Everything There Is." The problem is, science doesn't support that conclusion. How can something come from nothing? How can personal come from the impersonal? How can the intricacy, the design, the order, and the symmetry come about by chance?

Second, it violates logic as expressed in the laws of probability. In his book *The Church at the End of the Twentieth Century*, Francis Schaeffer tells of Murray Eden at MIT who was working with a high-speed computer to answer this question: "Beginning with chaos at any acceptable amount of time up to eight billion years ago, could the present complexity of the universe come about by chance? The answer was absolutely NO." And few scientists think the earth is significantly older than eight billion years. Four to four and a half billion years is a commonly accepted age. More recently, a British scientist named Hoyle, a mathematician and astronomer, calculated that it would take ten to the forty thousandth power years for chance to produce even the simplest cell. That is a length of time unimaginable, and so much older than the present universe as to discount any possibility of evolution being the answer to our universe.

A "futurist" speculating about what things would be like from the perspective of a scientist in the year 2090 wrote:

> It seems amazing now that there was a time when science was supposedly the "enemy" of faith, and religion was deemed hostile to technological investigation. The end of atheism and agnosticism became inevitable as soon as computer calculations made improbable the odds that random natural selection [the process central to the theory of evolution] could be the sole explanation for the ever increasing intricacies found in biology. Equally influential was the discovery of multiple universes, which astronomers found at the macrocosmic level and physicists detected in the microcosmic. Science thus established the current Age of Faith, re-creating the Creator. Nowadays, only the fool says in his heart, "There is no God." (*Time* magazine special issue, Fall 1992. "Kingdoms to Come," Richard Ostling, 61)

WHY I NEED TO KNOW THIS

1. If there is a God, then I must discover if I am accountable to Him.

2. I have an explanation for the existence and design of the universe.

3. I have answers for the great philosophical questions of meaning.

4. I have hope for meaning in life and for life after death.

5. I have a way of helping others. I have a background and information I can share with others when they are searching for answers in life.

Whenever you see something—anything—you are driven backward by experience and logic to ask, "Who created it?" When you get to original matter, you must ask who created it. At that point, if you stop and say, "No one. It is eternal. It has always been there," or if you say that "nothing" was in the beginning, and therefore, something came from nothing, that simply isn't believable to me. Believe it if you want to. Don't ask me to believe it. *It is no greater act of faith to believe in God than to believe what you must if you do not believe in God.*

2. The Order and Design in the World

Not only is the universe "here" and therefore has to be accounted for, the universe has order, design, and apparent purpose behind it. It is the difference between all the parts of a watch lying in a jumbled heap on a table, and having the watch all put together and running. It is one thing to have to explain where the jumble of parts came from. It is quite a greater thing to explain how they all got put together and working in such a way as to tell time. Not only is the universe "here," but also, it runs like a precision watch.

A brilliant scientist, Robert Jastrow, was a well-known geologist, physicist, and agnostic. Nevertheless, he wrote:

> Perhaps the appearance of life on earth is a miracle. Scientists are reluctant to accept that view, but their choices are limited. Either life was created on earth by a being outside the grasp of scientific understanding, or it evolved on our planet spontaneously through chemical reactions in non-living matter lying on the surface of the planet. The first theory places the question of the origin of life beyond the reach of scientific inquiry. It is a statement of faith in the power of a supreme being not subject to the laws of science. The second theory is also an act of faith. The act of faith consists in assuming that the scientific view of origins is correct without having any evidence to support that belief. ("God's Creation," *Science Digest*, Special Spring Issue, 1980, 68)

No, the scientists do not reject creation because the evidence demands it. It is just the opposite. They reject creation in spite of the fact that their answers for the universe are inadequate, but since they will not believe in God, the big bang and evolution are their only alternatives.

Were they to approach the data with an open mind, many more of them might find God a more satisfactory explanation for what we observe in the universe.

3. The Humanness of Humanity

Man is different from animals, and the cave drawings of thousands of years ago suggest that he has always considered himself to be different from the rest of creation. Man is different from non-man. He longs to know who he is. He longs to know where he came from. He longs to know where he is going. He longs for purpose and meaning in life while he is here on earth. Dogs and cats and monkeys have no longing for purpose. They have no longing for immortality. They have no thirst for a creator. Man has a conscience, a moral sense of right and wrong, superior intelligence, and a sense of a spiritual domain.

Man's religious nature clearly differentiates him from all other life on earth, and it is hard to explain except for the existence of God. If God did not exist, why would we ever have thought of Him? Evolutionists suggest that we invented the idea of God to explain the unexplainable. However, there are many other ways of explaining the unexplainable without relying on God. After all, scientists do it every day. In a sophisticated modern world, if we just once stamped out the idea of God and taught people a natural explanation to everything, it seems that the idea of God would simply fade away, never to be seen again.

People are incurably religious.

However, that has been tried, and it failed miserably. In Russia, religion was abolished in 1917. Communism was established as the official worldview, and atheism the official position on God. For seventy years, enforced with violent persecution and relentless brainwashing and education, the communists tried to eliminate the reflex for God.

What happened? A profound vacuum was created in the hearts of the Russian people. Communism fell under the weight of its own inadequacy, and the church has exploded in numbers, creating one of the most remarkable turnings to God in modern history. People are hungry for God in nearly every corner of Russian life. The atheism experiment is over. It failed. God is alive and well. People are incurably religious and are going to worship something. There has never been a culture in history that was not religious. There is nothing in the evolutionary process to explain this. The existence of God is the best explanation for it.

WHAT IS THE ROLE OF THE WILL
IN DECIDING ABOUT GOD?

We often believe what we want to believe regardless of the evidence.

If you have, for some reason, already decided that you do not want to believe in God, then you can find evidence to support your decision. But why would anyone do that? That is like deciding ahead of time that you don't have cancer, and therefore, you explain away all the evidence that might suggest you do. What you *think* about whether or not you have cancer is irrelevant. The only thing that is relevant is whether or not you *have* it. Therefore, the only safe course of action for you is to look at all the evidence, and believe the evidence, not your presupposition.

> **The issue of God's existence is more than an idle debate.**

If all this is a matter of intellectual curiosity, we can debate it until we run out of energy, end in a stalemate, shrug our shoulders, and say, "Well, that was interesting, but I guess there's no way to know the answer for sure." Then we can go home and think about something else.

But it is certainly more than an intellectual debate to me. I want to know if there is a God. I want to know if it is safe to die. I want to know if there is something I can do to make everything okay when they lay me six feet under and throw a shovelful of dirt in my face.

In addition, I want to know if it is safe to live. I want to know if there is purpose and meaning in life. I want to know if I am going through life on my own, at the mercy of random blows of fate, or if there is a God who loves me and will guide me and look out for me. I want to know if there is someone I can pray to, or if I am alone. I want to know if there is such a thing as truth and error, right and wrong. When I lose my job, when my family falls apart, when my health fails, when the wrong person is elected, when my home is devastated by a tornado or my town is ravaged by a flood, is there a God? Will He see me through the trials of life? Is it safe to live?

I'm not going to jeopardize my eternal destiny or present sense of meaning and purpose in life by deciding ahead of time that there is no God, and then interpreting all the evidence in light of that presupposition. I'm going to look at the evidence with an open mind and let the evidence tell me whether or not there is a God. When I do this, I end up saying, "God, I believe in You." There isn't a single logical flaw in that decision, and there isn't a single body of information or evidence to suggest convincingly that it isn't probable.

There is an extremely high percentage of people in the United States who claim to believe in God. However, when you compare that fact with the lifestyles of many Americans, it is difficult to reconcile their belief with their actions and values. John 14:21 makes it clear that the mark of *loving* God is *obeying* Him. If the 85 percent or so of the people in the United States who claim to *believe in* God were also *obeying* Him, we would not be witnessing the breathtaking moral decline that we see in America. Using the biblical criterion of obedience to God, it would be difficult to validate that 85 percent of the people in America take God very seriously. The real percentage would be disappointingly lower than that, I fear.

People's actions and values must match their beliefs.

So why don't more people want to truly know God— know Him in the way the Bible says: "He who has My commandments and keeps them, it is he who loves Me. . . . If you keep My commandments, you will abide in My love" (John 14:21; 15:10)? There are certainly many reasons people would give for not seeking God more fully. One reason, however, is that they don't *want* to meet Him. They don't want to be placed under the demands God would place them under. It has not so much to do with the validity of external evidence, but rather with the fact that they are unwilling to repent and place their lives under the control of God.

If people really wanted to know God, they would search for Him in ways that are likely to lead to Him. Since, if the God of the Bible exists, He requires things from us, then you must start your search for Him with a heart prepared for repentance and obedience. If there is a God, do you think you can meet Him and then tell *Him* what to do? No, when we meet God, we must be prepared for Him to tell *us* what to do. And we must be prepared to do it. No one can say he has examined all the evidence about God if he has not sought God in ways appropriate to finding Him.

The true barrier to knowing God is our "will." We are unwilling to give ourselves over to Him, which is what He requires of those who would know Him. Repentance and obedience are the key elements of a search for God. And when we find God, we discover that it was He who found us. Apart from God's grace, we don't want to know Him. He places in our hearts the desire to know Him. He leads us in our search. When we come to love God, we discover that it was He who first loved us. It is God Himself who gives us the desire to know Him.

God leads us in our search for Him.

Do you want to know God? That is an exciting thing. It is an indication that God Himself, the Creator of the universe, is knocking on the door of *your* life. In a spirit of repentance and obedience, let Him in. Tell Him that you believe in Him. Tell Him that you are willing to repent of your sins, and that you want Him to come into your life and help you become the kind of person He wants you to be. Then, read the Scriptures, pray as best you know how, get involved in a church that teaches the Bible, and continue your pursuit of God. He will reveal Himself continuously to you for the rest of your life.

CONCLUSION

Whatever we believe, we believe by faith. If we believe in God, we believe by faith. If we do not believe in God, we are still exercising faith. Why believe in God? Because He is the most reasonable explanation for the existence of the universe; its complexity, purpose, and design; and the uniqueness of humanity. If we want to believe in Him, there is ample evidence to do so.

SPEED BUMP!

Slow down to be sure you've gotten the main points from the chapter.

Q1. Why would someone not believe in God?

A1. Some people reject God because the world is *inconsistent* with their concept of God.

Q2. Why would someone believe in God?

A2. People accept God because the existence of God is the best *explanation* for the world as it is.

Q3. What is the role of the will in deciding about God?

A3. We often believe what we want to believe regardless of the *evidence*.

FILL IN THE BLANK

Q1. Why would someone not believe in God?

A1. Some people reject God because the world is _____ with their concept of God.

Q2. Why would someone believe in God?

A2. People accept God because the existence of God is the best _____ for the world as it is.

Q3. What is the role of the will in deciding about God?

A3. We often believe what we want to believe regardless of the _____.

FOR FURTHER THOUGHT AND DISCUSSION

1. Did you believe in God before you read this chapter? If you did, why did you? Did this chapter add to the reasons why you believed, or merely confirm why you already believed?

2. If you did not believe in God before reading this chapter, how has this information affected your perspective?

3. Name another reason to believe God exists.

4. If a child wanted to know about God and you wanted to tell him that God exists, what would you tell him?

5. How could your family history and experience influence your belief in God and what He might be like? How would it affect your ability to trust God?

WHAT IF I DON'T BELIEVE?

There are several common personal consequences of not believing in the existence of God.

1. You are forced to explain the existence and design of the universe with the equation: Nothing + The Impersonal + Time + Chance = Everything There Is.

2. You have no answers to the classic questions of meaning for man: Who am I? Where did I come from? Why am I here? Where am I going?

3. The past is viewed as a meaningless accident, and death is viewed as meaningless annihilation. If you are sandwiched between a meaningless past and meaningless future, you cannot escape a meaningless present.

FOR FURTHER STUDY

1. Scripture

There are at least seven major passages in the Bible that speak of reasons to believe in God. They are:

- Job 38:1—39:30
- Psalm 19:1–6
- Ecclesiastes 3:11
- Isaiah 40:12–17
- Isaiah 40:26
- Acts 14:17
- Romans 1:18–20

Read these passages and consider how they integrate with arguments for God's existence.

2. Books

There are several other books that can be helpful in studying further this subject:
My God, Michael Green
Finding God in Unexpected Places, Philip Yancey
Enjoying the Presence of God, Martyn Lloyd-Jones
The God Who Is There, Francis Schaeffer

CHAPTER **3**

WHY BELIEVE THAT JESUS IS GOD?

Immortal Love, forever full,
Forever flowing free,
Forever shared, forever whole,
A never-ebbing sea!
—**John Greenleaf Whittier**

The life of Jesus split history like a blinding lightning flash on a hot July night. Everything that has ever happened is now measured as having happened either before Christ or after Christ. Concerning His life, Philip Yancey wrote in *The Jesus I Never Knew,*

> Richard Nixon got carried away with excitement in 1969 when Apollo astronauts first landed on the moon. "It's the greatest day since creation!" crowed the president, until Billy Graham solemnly reminded him of Christmas and Easter. By any measure of history, Graham was right. This Galilean, who in his lifetime spoke to fewer people than would fill just one of the many stadia Graham has filled, changed the world more than any other person. He introduced a new force field into history, and now holds the allegiance of a third of all the people on earth.
>
> Today, people even use Jesus' name to curse by. How strange it would sound if, when a businessman missed a golf putt, he yelled, "Thomas Jefferson!" or if a plumber screamed "Mahatma Gandhi!" when his pipe wrench smashed a finger. We cannot get away from this man Jesus.
>
> "More than 1900 years later," said H.G. Wells, "a historian like myself, who doesn't even call himself a Christian, finds the picture centering irresistibly around the life and character of this most significant man. . . . The historian's test of an individual's greatness is 'What did he leave to grow?' Did he start men to thinking along fresh lines with a vigor that persisted after him? By this test Jesus stands first." You can gauge the size of a ship that has passed out of sight by the huge wake it leaves behind. (16–17)

No one has left behind a greater wake than Jesus. No one who has ever lived has ever come close to this remarkable person. But who was He? Many people agree that He was a great moral teacher, but is that all? Could anyone who said the things Jesus said be considered merely a great moral teacher? He claimed to be God, to be able to forgive sins, and to be the only way to heaven. If He is not God, He is certainly not merely a great moral teacher. C. S. Lewis, a devoted Christian scholar of an earlier generation, once wrote penetrating words that strike to the heart of the issue:

> I am trying here to prevent anyone saying the really foolish thing that people often say about [Jesus]: "I'm ready to accept Jesus as a great moral teacher, but I don't accept His claim to be God." That is the one thing we must not say. A man who . . . said the sort of things Jesus said would not be a great moral teacher. He would either be a lunatic—on a level with the man who says he is a poached egg—or else he would be the Devil of Hell. You must make your choice. Either this man was, and is, the Son of God: or else a madman or something worse. You can shut Him up for a fool, you can spit at Him and kill Him as a demon; or you can fall at His feet and call Him Lord and God. But let us not come with any patronizing nonsense about His being a great human teacher. He has not left that open to us. He did not intend to. (*Mere Christianity*, 56)

No, Jesus was not merely a great moral teacher. Josh McDowell, in his book *Evidence That Demands a Verdict*, made a similar point. Jesus is either a liar, a lunatic, or the Lord. That is, either He was not God and He knew He was not, in which case He was a liar, or He was not God but He thought He was, in which case He was a lunatic, or He was God, in which case He is the Lord.

The decision is a monumental one, because if Jesus' words are true, our response determines our eternal destiny. Central to the Christian faith is the belief that Jesus was/is God, and as Yancey said, today, a third of the people on earth believe it.

Why?

There are at least five reasons why Christians believe Jesus was God.

DOES THE BIBLE CLAIM THAT JESUS WAS GOD?

The Bible makes clear that Jesus was God.

Scripture states clearly that Jesus was God. John 1:1 says, "In the beginning was the Word, and the Word was with God, and the Word was God." In Titus 2:13, the apostle Paul wrote of the second coming of Christ, that we should be "looking for the blessed hope and glorious appearing of our great God and Savior Jesus Christ," clearly stating that Jesus is both God and Savior. Finally, in 1 John 5:20, the apostle John wrote of Jesus who is the "true God."

In addition, Jesus Himself claimed to be God. He said, "Before Abraham was, I AM" (John 8:58). I AM is the name of God, sometimes translated Jehovah or Yahweh. To a Jew, it was the name of God that no one dared to speak because it was God's personal name. It was the name God revealed to Moses from out of the burning bush on Mt. Sinai. Jews did not speak the name out of fear that doing so might inadvertently lead them to blaspheme. Because of that statement, the Jews picked up stones to throw at Jesus (verse 59). Why? Because the penalty for blaspheming was death by stoning. There was certainly no question in the minds of the ones who heard Him that He was claiming to be God.

On another occasion He said, "I and My Father are one" (John 10:30). The religious leaders of the day understood Jesus' claim to deity. They said, "We have a law, and according to our law He ought to die, because He made Himself the Son of God" (John 19:7). The only reason Jesus' claim to be the Son of God would carry the death penalty is if it were a claim of deity. The high priest asked Jesus directly, "I [solemnly urge] You by the living God, that You tell us whether You are the Christ, the Son of God" (Matthew 26:63 NASB). Jesus replied, "It is as you said" (verse 64). When the high priest heard this he cried (for all practical purposes), "OFF WITH HIS HEAD!" Then others around Him spit in His face and beat Him. Why? In their eyes, He was a blasphemer. He claimed to be God. Nothing else could account for the response and reaction of the religious leaders.

If we take the Scripture at face value, we have no reason to doubt that Jesus is God.

IN THIS CHAPTER WE LEARN THAT . . .

1. The Bible makes clear that Jesus was God.

2. Jesus fulfilled all prophecies necessary to qualify as the Messiah.

3. The words that Jesus spoke went beyond the words of a mere man, and were divine.

4. The deeds that Jesus did went beyond the deeds of a mere man, and were divine.

5. Both the Bible and history confirm that Jesus rose from the dead.

DID JESUS FULFILL PROPHECY?

Jesus fulfilled all prophecies necessary to qualify as the Messiah.

God promised the father of all Jews, Abraham, that all the world would be blessed through him. No one thinks that the blessing was to come through Abraham during his lifetime, but that it would happen through a descendant or descendants of Abraham. And, while many blessings have come through the Jewish nation, everyone pretty much agrees there was more to come.

Then, King David, one of the great heroes of Israel, was given a promise that has given hope to the ages: "I will raise up your offspring to succeed you . . . and I will establish his kingdom. . . . I will establish the throne of his kingdom forever" (2 Samuel 7:12–13 NIV).

No king or succession of kings ever fulfilled that prophecy. All hope rested on the expectation that in the future, someone would.

Later, the prophet Isaiah hinted that this one who is to come has not been forgotten.

> Therefore the Lord Himself will give you a sign: Behold, the virgin shall conceive and bear a Son, and shall call His name Immanuel. (Isaiah 7:14)

The apostle Matthew told us that Immanuel means "God with us" (Matthew 1:23)—no small coincidence.

Isaiah went on to describe in remarkable detail the contribution that this one who was "God with us" would make:

> Behold, my servant shall prosper . . .
> And shall be very high. . . .
> [He shall] startle many nations . . .
> for that which has not been told them they shall see,
> and that which they have not heard they shall understand. . . .
> He was despised and rejected by men;
> a man of sorrows, and acquainted with grief;
> and as one from whom men hide their faces
> he was despised, and we esteemed him not.
> Surely he has borne our griefs
> and carried our sorrows;
> yet we esteemed him stricken,
> smitten by God, and afflicted.

But he was wounded for our transgressions,
he was bruised for our iniquities;
upon him was the chastisement that made us whole,
and with his stripes we are healed.
All we like sheep have gone astray;
we have turned every one to his own way;
and the LORD has laid on him the iniquity of us all.
(Isaiah 52:13—53:6 RSV)

Though Israel waited and hoped, no one in its history had ever fulfilled that remarkable prophecy.

The one they waited for would even be born in a specific place:

But you, Bethlehem Ephrathah,
Though you are little among the thousands of Judah,
Yet out of you shall come forth to Me
The One to be Ruler in Israel,
Whose goings forth are from of old,
From everlasting. (Micah 5:2)

When we look at the life of Jesus, we see that He fulfilled these prophecies. All the nations of the world have been blessed in Him. He was the son of David, and will rule forever on His throne. He was born in Bethlehem. He was born of a virgin and called Immanuel. He was despised by men and rejected. He was wounded for our sins; the Lord did lay on Him the iniquity of us all. Was this some vast coincidence? Or was it possible that the story of Jesus began, not in a manger in Bethlehem, but in the heart of God in eternity past, hinted at by the prophecies of the Old Testament?

DID JESUS SPEAK DIVINE WORDS?

The words that Jesus spoke went beyond the words of a mere man, and were divine.

The words that Jesus spoke went so far beyond what any mere mortal has ever spoken that they set Him apart from all others who have ever lived. The character of His moral code, the unexpectedness of His teachings, and the authority of His commandments put Him in a league by Himself—the league of the divine.

His teachings form the loftiest moral code ever heard. "Do unto others as you would have others do unto you." Love your neighbor as yourself—but not only your neighbor—love your enemy, and pray for those who despitefully use you. If someone strikes you on one cheek, turn to him the other also. If someone wrongs you, forgive him seventy times seven times.

His description of reality is upside down:

Blessed are the poor in spirit,
For theirs is the kingdom of heaven.
Blessed are those who mourn,
For they shall be comforted.
Blessed are the meek,
For they shall inherit the earth.
Blessed are those who hunger and thirst for righteousness,
For they shall be filled.
Blessed are the merciful,
For they shall obtain mercy.
Blessed are the pure in heart,
For they shall see God.
Blessed are the peacemakers,
For they shall be called sons of God.
Blessed are those who are persecuted for righteousness' sake,
For theirs is the kingdom of heaven. (Matthew 5:3–10)

Who would think that the poor in spirit, mourners, meek, spiritually hungry and thirsty, merciful, pure in heart, peacemakers, and persecuted are blessed? For the most part, these are conditions we don't want. But in the kingdom of God, the one who loses his life finds it. So blessed is the one who loses his life. The first shall be last and the last shall be first, so blessed are those who are last. It is all backward. Eternal reality is backward.

Someone said that if Jesus had never lived, we could never have invented Him. What He did and what He said are so foreign to our nature that it would never have occurred to any human being to come up with such an unexpected person.

This is another mark of His divinity.

In addition to the character and quality of His words, the subject of His words mark Jesus as divine. He taught, not of His own kingdom, but of the kingdom of God. This kingdom was not what His countrymen wanted to hear, however. They wanted a charismatic military/political leader who would galvanize the country around himself and lead them to military victory over their Roman oppressors. When Jesus began to speak to them of the kingdom of God, people flocked to Him, hoping for the best (in their view). They didn't get it. What they got instead was an eyebrow-raising description of how they ought to live while under Roman oppression. Michael Green wrote of this life in his marvelous volume *Who Is This Jesus?*

> It is a life of attractive goodness, quite different from the long-faced ethics of the religious. It will be like salt giving savor to a dish of food or a light giving direction to folk fumbling around in the dark. People in the kingdom will realize that the wish is father of the deed, and therefore that hatred is as obnoxious to God as murder, and lust as adultery. Divorce is not the way of the kingdom: God made the two to be—and remain—one flesh, and everything else is a fall from that ideal. The disciple is to be marked in several ways. His word will be his bond—no need for flowery oaths. Forgiveness will be his way of life, even when wronged. Love, even love for his enemies, will be the supreme mark of the follower of Jesus.
>
> [The member of the kingdom of God is to] live a life of generosity, of modesty, of prayer. He will not show off. He will not hoard his money but will give a lot of it away, for his real investment is in heaven. He will be totally single-hearted, and his life will be marked by a marvelous peace. After all, God looks after the flowers and the grass and the birds. Can He not be trusted to look after us? What then is the point of worrying?
>
> But nobody drifts into this wonderful kingdom that Jesus came to usher in. You have to ask, to seek, to knock. You have to enter through a narrow gate. You have to build your very life on the rock of Jesus. (32–33)

After articulating the differences between the kingdom of the world and the kingdom of heaven, Jesus called His hearers to follow Him. He said, essentially, this world has nothing to offer you. The kingdom of God has everything to offer you. You can live life God's way with His blessing, or your way without it. What will you do? You must decide.

Are these the words of a man? Think about it. Who is the greatest thinker and speaker who ever lived? Socrates? Plato? Thomas Aquinas? Gandhi? Think about it. Anything any one of them has said falls so far short of what Jesus said that it is like comparing a monkey to Einstein. Their words fall so short of the character and tone and authority of Jesus' words. These are not the words of a man. They are the words of God.

DID JESUS DO DIVINE DEEDS?

The deeds that Jesus did went beyond the deeds of a mere man, and were divine.

In 1 Corinthians 4:20, the apostle Paul wrote, "The kingdom of God is not a matter of talk but of power" (NIV). Jesus said, if you don't believe because of My words, believe because of the deeds I do (John 10:37–38).

As the crowds gathered around Jesus, hanging on His words, there were those who needed some verification of His message. Jesus realized this, and matched the power of His words with the power of His deeds. His goal was to call people to repent and believe in Him. But if His actions could reinforce His message, He was ready to act. When people were sick or diseased, He healed them. If they were blind, He gave them sight. If they were possessed of demons, He drove the demons out.

WHY I NEED TO KNOW THIS

If I don't know and understand that Jesus was God, I have no understanding of what true Christianity is all about. I am out of touch with the message of the New Testament and the teachings of Christ. If I don't know that Jesus is God, I am not yet a Christian, my sins have not yet been forgiven, and I have no assurance of life after death.

There were a number of reasons why Jesus performed these miracles. One, of course, is that He had compassion on the people who came to Him with their miseries. He cared deeply about the people He ministered to. Second, He performed the miracles to validate His message. He claimed to be the light of the world, and to demonstrate it, He gave sight to a blind man. He claimed to be the bread of life, and to demonstrate it, He fed thousands. He claimed to be the resurrection and the life, and to demonstrate it, He raised a man from the dead. His miracles were not stunts to draw publicity. They were implicit claims to deity. Third, His physical healings were a sign of His ability to heal spiritually. He told a paralytic to rise up and walk. Then He asked the crowd, is it easier to say "your sins are forgiven you," or to say "rise up and walk"? The answer, of course, is that it is easier to say "your sins are forgiven you." How is anyone going to know if it is true? So, to demonstrate that He had power to forgive sins, He told the paralytic to rise up and walk.

Finally, His miracles forced the witnesses to make a decision about Him. You were forced to decide whether you believed that Jesus was who He said He was. If He were not God, how could His miracles be explained? If they could not be explained, why would you not accept Him as God?

Whom do you know who can perform miracles? Each of His miracles was a claim to divinity. John the Baptist wrote a letter and asked if Jesus was the one who was to come (meaning the Messiah) or was there another. Jesus' reply was, "Go and report to John what you hear and see: the blind receive sight and the lame walk, the lepers are cleansed and the deaf hear, the dead are raised up, and the poor have the gospel preached to them. And blessed is he who does not take offense at Me" (Matthew 11:4–6 NASB).

Are miracles the deeds of man? Think of the greatest world leaders you have ever known about. Has anyone done anything to match Jesus? Julius Caesar? Alexander the Great? Napoleon? Abraham Lincoln? Think about it. Anything any of them has done falls so far short of what Jesus did that it is like comparing a boxing kangaroo to a neurosurgeon. Their deeds fall so short of the actions of Jesus, they cannot be in the same category of being. The things Jesus did are not the deeds of a man. They are the deeds of God.

DID JESUS RISE FROM THE DEAD?

Both the Bible and history confirm that Jesus rose from the dead.

Jesus definitely died on the cross. Hundreds, perhaps thousands, of people witnessed it. The Romans were not careless executioners; they knew when a person was dead. They had ways of making sure. They broke the legs of the person so he could not support himself to breathe any more, and he asphyxiated. But Jesus needed no bones broken. He was already dead. To be sure, the Roman speared His side. No reaction. Blood and water came out, a sign of legal death. The executioner had to verify the death to Pilate. If he had gotten it wrong, it would have meant his death. Finally, if those certain events had never happened, a historian would have corrected the lie. Jesus definitely died.

They buried Him just before the Sabbath. Three days later, the disciples went to the tomb and found it empty. There was no one to deny it. All anyone would have had to do to put an end to the rumor was to produce the body. They could not.

> **The disciples would not have given their lives to a lie.**

There are only two possibilities—either the tomb was empty or it was not. If it was not, the Christian claim would have been stomped out immediately. So, it was empty. If it was empty, there are two possibilities. Someone stole the body, or else Jesus rose from the dead.

Who would have wanted the body? Jesus' enemies? No. They wanted Him in the grave. They wouldn't have stolen it. Would His friends have wanted the body? Perhaps, but they would not have tried to steal it, and if they had they would have failed.

The disciples did not understand the resurrection until afterward. They were not expecting Him to rise. Additionally, had they tried to steal His body, the Roman guard would have prevented it. Finally, the disciples would not have dedicated their lives and paid with their lives for spreading the gospel to the ends of the earth if they had known the resurrection was a lie.

If Jesus' body was not removed by His enemies or His friends, the answer that remains is that He rose from the dead, just as He said He would (Matthew 28:6).

Jesus met with His followers over the next forty days, and then ascended into heaven—an event that was witnessed by many. After that the church grew by the thousands. How do we explain the explosion of the early church? The first disciples had scattered like quail before hunters when Jesus was crucified. Some had gone back home to Galilee. But now, they could not be silenced. What made the difference? If the resurrection could have been refuted, would thousands of Jews have risked being cut off from family and regular Jewish society?

When you look at the facts of the resurrection, without having made up your mind ahead of time against it, the birth, explosive growth, and permanent survival of the church are powerful evidence for the truth of the resurrection.

CONCLUSION

If the resurrection is true, the implications are staggering. First, we can be sure that Jesus was who He claimed to be. The apostle Paul wrote, "[He] was born of the seed of David according to the flesh, and declared to be the Son of God . . . by the resurrection from the dead" (Romans 1:3–4).

Second, if Jesus rose from the dead, we can be sure that everything else He said was true. Most importantly, He did make possible the forgiveness of our sins and the gift of eternal life. Again, the apostle Paul wrote, "He was delivered over to death for our sins and was raised to life for our justification" (Romans 4:25 NIV).

Third, if He rose from the dead, we can be assured of our own resurrection and eternal life. "If Christ is not risen, your faith is futile; you are still in your sins!" (1 Corinthians 15:17). But if Christ has risen, our faith is not futile and we are not still in our sins. And, it is as Jesus said in John 14:2–3:

> In My Father's house are many mansions; if it were not so, I would have told you. I go to prepare a place for you. And if I go and prepare a place for you, I will come again and receive you to Myself; that where I am, there you may be also.

If Jesus has been raised from the dead, if He has been raised to a new and deathless life, then best of all, He is still alive!

Why believe that Jesus was God? Because of the prophecies He fulfilled, because of the character of His words, because of the character of His deeds, and because of the resurrection.

Napoleon is reputed to have said,

> I marvel that whereas the ambitious dreams of myself, Caesar, Alexander, should have vanished into thin air, a Judean peasant, Jesus, should be able to stretch His hands across the destinies of men and nations.
>
> I know men; and I tell you that Jesus Christ is no mere man. Between him and every other person in the world there is no possible term of comparison. Alexander, Caesar, Charlemagne, and I myself have founded empires; but upon what do these creations of our genius depend? Upon force. Jesus alone founded his empire upon love; and to this very day millions would die for him.

SPEED BUMP!

Slow down to be sure you've gotten the main points from this chapter.

Q1. Does the Bible claim that Jesus was God?

A1. The Bible makes *clear* that Jesus was God.

Q2. Did Jesus fulfill prophecy?

A2. Jesus *fulfilled* all prophecies necessary to qualify as the Messiah.

Q3. Did Jesus speak divine words?

A3. The words that Jesus spoke went *beyond* the words of a mere man, and were divine.

Q4. Did Jesus do divine deeds?

A4. The deeds that Jesus did went *beyond* the deeds of a mere man, and were divine.

Q5. Did Jesus rise from the dead?

A5. Both the Bible and history *confirm* that Jesus rose from the dead.

FILL IN THE BLANK

Q1. Does the Bible claim that Jesus was God?

A1. The Bible makes _____ that Jesus was God.

Q2. Did Jesus fulfill prophecy?

A2. Jesus _____ all prophecies necessary to qualify as the Messiah.

Q3. Did Jesus speak divine words?

A3. The words that Jesus spoke went _____ the words of a mere man, and were divine.

Q4. Did Jesus do divine deeds?

A4. The deeds that Jesus did went _____ the deeds of a mere man, and were divine.

Q5. Did Jesus rise from the dead?

A5. Both the Bible and history _____ that Jesus rose from the dead.

FOR FURTHER THOUGHT AND DISCUSSION

1. Why do you think most people consider Jesus to be merely a great moral teacher even though, if that were true, many of the things He said would have to be either lies or lunacy?

2. Some people claim that Jesus manipulated circumstances in His life so that He came out looking like He fulfilled messianic prophecies even though He was not the Messiah. What is your reaction to that?

3. Do you think there is a relationship between many of the miracles Jesus did and the things He was saying? If so, what do you think the relationship is?

WHAT IF I DON'T BELIEVE?

1. If Jesus is not God, I must admit that the Bible is full of lies.

2. If Jesus is not the Savior of mankind, He cannot forgive sins, and I have no way of dealing with sins.

3. Someone might say that if Jesus is not God, I don't need to concern myself over following His teachings, and that would be true. But my sense of guilt and shame over things done wrong would still trouble me.

4. I have no hope of life after death, and no assurance of guidance in this life.

5. I can ignore His teachings about right and wrong, and thus I can do whatever society will let me get away with. On the other hand, others can do to me whatever society will let them get away with. The law of the jungle prevails—the survival of the fittest or the luckiest.

WHAT IF I DO BELIEVE?

1. I can have the confidence that the Bible is not full of lies. I can trust it for guidance in this life and into the next.

2. If Jesus is God, the Bible can be trusted, and I have hope that my sins can be forgiven.

3. There is such a thing as right and wrong, and I can look to Jesus not only for eternal life but also for guidance and strength to do right in this life.

FOR FURTHER STUDY

1. Scripture

There are several Scriptures that speak of the deity of Christ. They include:

- Mark 2:28
- John 1:1–14
- John 8:58
- John 20:28
- Philippians 2:9–11

Read these passages and consider how they contribute to our understanding of man's need for God.

2. Books

There are several other books that will be very helpful in studying this subject further:

The Jesus I Never Knew, Philip Yancey

Who Is This Jesus? Michael Green

Mere Christianity, C. S. Lewis

The Words and Works of Jesus Christ, J. Dwight Pentecost

CHAPTER **4**

WHY BELIEVE THE BIBLE IS TRUE?

*The Bible is not the kind of a book
a man would write if he could
or could write if he would.*
—Lewis Sperry Chafer

J ust west of Colorado Springs, Pikes Peak looms vast and imposing over the central Colorado landscape. Its rounded bulk rises more than fourteen thousand feet into the thin, arid sky, dominating the view of anyone within scores of miles. "Pikes Peak or Bust!" was the cry of westward-bound pioneers because of the gold and other minerals discovered in the area, such as the Cripple Creek gold field to the southwest. From its commanding heights, Katherine Bates wrote:

> O beautiful for spacious skies,
> For amber waves of grain,
> For purple mountain majesties
> Above the fruited plain!

I remember standing there one breezy summer day scanning the horizon, and there they were: spacious skies, purple mountain majesties, and fruited plains. I'm not sure it was the right time of the year for amber waves of grain. One easily could have thrown in deep blue mountain lakes, high meadows, cavernous hidden valleys, and stunning sunsets or sunrises. In the early days of our nation, travelers going west had to detour hundreds of miles around the southern boundary of the peak and its related mountains. It is a breathtaking sight, and one can easily imagine what inspired Ms. Bates to pen such eloquent and timeless words.

From the heights of the massive projection, one can see to the farthest horizon in 360 degrees. When you scan the horizon from anywhere within central Colorado, Pikes Peak is the dominant presence.

IN THIS CHAPTER WE LEARN THAT . . .

1. The Bible claims to be the Word of God, without error.

2. Ancient manuscripts, archaeology, and prophecy all support the reliability of the Bible.

3. The Bible accurately describes humanity as inherently flawed and without ability to correct itself.

4. The Bible has had a positive influence on humanity wherever it has been known and followed.

In the same way, when we scan the horizon of human civilization for the last two thousand years, we see the Bible, confronting the traveler like a massive mountain that must be negotiated and cannot be wished away. The Bible is an enormous historical presence, the dominant piece of literature and a dominant influence in history since the time of Christ. No other piece of literature has come close to its impact. If the Bible is a mighty oak, then every other piece of literature is a sapling or a seedling.

A curious, earnest traveler on life's highway would want to know about and seriously consider the claims of such a book. Is the Bible true? Is it the Word of God? Do its words have any claim on my life?

The answer to these questions often lies in one's assumptions. If you assume that it is possible that the Bible might be the Word of God and go where the evidence takes you, there is compelling evidence to believe that the Bible is true, that it is the Word of God, that it does have claim on your life. If you don't assume that possibility, then there is not enough evidence to overcome your assumption.

So if anyone really wants to know if the Bible is true, he must be prepared to accept the possibility. Otherwise, there is no use looking into it. He already has his answer. However, if anyone wants to investigate with an open mind the credibility of the Bible, there are a number of issues that can be compelling.

WHAT CLAIM DOES THE BIBLE MAKE FOR ITSELF?

The Bible claims to be the Word of God, without error.

If God exists and if we are to know anything about Him, He must have revealed Himself to us in some reliable way. The Bible claims to be the revelation of God to humanity. Throughout the Old Testament, we read "Thus saith the Lord." That fact is verified in Acts 4:25, where we read, "You [God] spoke by the Holy Spirit through the mouth of your servant, our father David" (NIV). In 2 Timothy 3:16, we read, "All Scripture is given by inspiration of God, and is profitable for doctrine, for reproof, for correction, for instruction in righteousness," and in 2 Peter 1:20–21, we read, "No prophecy of Scripture is of any private interpretation, for prophecy never came by the will of man, but holy men of God spoke as they were moved by the Holy Spirit." Lending credibility to all that, Jesus said, "Till heaven and earth pass away, one jot or one tittle will by no means pass from the law till all is fulfilled" (Matthew 5:18). The jot and tittle were the smallest characters of the Hebrew alphabet.

WHY I NEED TO KNOW THIS

I need to know this because I need some reason to believe that the Bible can be trusted. It is true that often we believe or do not believe the Bible simply because we have decided to or not to. However, God asks no one to believe anything unreasonable. He asks no one to believe nonsense. He asks no one to believe on the basis of "nothing." All faith is based on truth, reality, and reasonable conclusions. When we realize this, it can strengthen our faith and our resolve to live as we ought.

If we are to have a reliable knowledge of God, we must have a reliable Bible. People often are told or get the impression that there are errors or contradictions in the Bible, but things that seem to be errors or contradictions can be explained. For example, the four Gospels differ in their account as to what was written on a sign that was nailed to the cross above Jesus' head when He was crucified. Matthew says, "This is Jesus, the king of the Jews." Mark says, "The king of the Jews." Luke says, "This is the king of the Jews," and John says, "Jesus of Nazareth the king of the Jews." True, all of these are different. However, none of these accounts say that this was all that was written on the sign. The whole thing can be reconciled by realizing that the sign contained everything that was written: "This is Jesus of Nazareth the king of the Jews." From this full statement, each author, for reasons of his own, articulated only part of the statement, but there is no error.

Clark Pinnock, in *Set Forth Your Case*, has written:

The [supposed] "errors" of the Bible are a very slippery lot. Just when you have your hands on one, it evades you and disappears. At bottom, these "errors" are really only *difficulties masquerading as errors*. In 1800 the French Institute in Paris issued a list of eighty-two errors in the Bible which they believed would destroy Christianity. Today none of these "errors" remain! With further reflection and new discoveries, these "errors" were cleared away. Surely it will be so with all such difficulties. We have our Saviour's word for that. (102)

To be sure, there may be some difficulties with the inerrancy of the Bible, but until the Bible interpreter is omniscient and all the information is in, we need not be intimidated by the allegation that there are any mistakes in the Bible. Difficulties in Scripture do not overthrow the fact that in the original writings, the Scripture was without error. They are only mountains yet to be climbed.

WHY DO WE BELIEVE THE BIBLE IS RELIABLE?

Ancient manuscripts, archaeology, and prophecy all support the reliability of the Bible.

It is one thing to say the Bible is the accurate record of the word of God in the original manuscripts, but two questions rise. First, are the manuscripts we have today reliable copies of the original, and second, is there any evidence to suggest it's true that the Bible is the Word of God? There are comforting answers to both these questions.

Ancient Manuscripts

There are some discrepancies in the various ancient manuscripts, but those discrepancies are insignificant, and have no bearing on any doctrine. For example, some of the discrepancies are like the difference between spelling the word *color* as "c-o-l-o-r," the way we do now, or spelling it "c-o-l-o-u-r," an acceptable variation. Those kinds of discrepancies exist. There are also some discrepancies in numbers, but they are easily explained. They are like an ancient scribe putting too many zeros in a number, writing 1000 when it should have been 100, for example.

There may be an existing manuscript that is exactly like the original, but we don't know for sure, because if two manuscripts vary, we do not know for sure which one is more like the original.

To reiterate, however, the number of these variances are very few, and they affect no doctrine. After two thousand years of copying (which had to be done, or else only one person in the world would have a Bible, assuming it hadn't rotted into oblivion by now), Bruce Metzger, a renowned New Testament scholar who taught at Princeton, has said that of the twenty thousand lines in the New Testament, only forty are up for debate today. Everything else is a given, and none of the variances affect the Christian faith.

There are two other matters that are important in establishing the reliability of the ancient manuscript from which we get our English Bible. First, there are many of them. Going back to secular documents that were written roughly during the same time frame as the New Testament, for example, there are only seven copies of Plato's *Tetrologies*, ten copies of Caesar's *Gaelic Wars*, and 643 copies of Homer's *Iliad*. There are over five thousand ancient manuscripts of the New Testament! In addition to the New Testament documents, we have over ten thousand ancient manuscripts or parts of manuscripts of the Old Testament. Of course, the more manuscripts you have, the easier it is to verify the truth and accuracy of the manuscripts, and the more certain it is that you know what the original document said. The Bible is easily the most numerous ancient document in existence, and by comparing this galaxy of manuscripts, we see that they all say exactly the same thing, with minor exceptions. Our Bible today is reliable.

A third matter validating the credibility of the manuscripts we have is how old the manuscripts are. That is, how close to the original is the oldest manuscript we have? The New Testament manuscripts are far superior to other ancient writings when comparing the time lapse between the earliest existing copy and the original writing. For example, Caesar's *Gaelic Wars* was written about 60 BC, yet the earliest existing manuscript we have is dated AD 900, nearly one thousand years later. Plato's *Tetrologies* was written in about 400 BC but the earliest manuscript we have of it dates to about AD 900, nearly thirteen hundred years older. And Homer's *Iliad* was written about 900 BC, but the earliest copy we have dates to about 400 BC, some five hundred years older. While the New Testament

Thousands of ancient manuscripts are in agreement.

was written during the first century, completed no later than AD 100, the earliest known manuscript that contains most of the New Testament dates to about AD 200, a span of only about one hundred years. And there are fragments dating back as early as AD 125, and recently a fragment of the New Testament was found dating to before AD 100, during the lifetime of the apostle John.

There is one final piece of information that needs to be added to the credibility of the Bible manuscripts. Many people have heard of the Dead Sea Scrolls but often do not know why they are so important. These scrolls were found in a series of caves in 1947 in a desolate area just west of the Dead Sea. The place was inhabited by a narrow sect of the Jewish community between 145 BC and AD 68. For some reason, many of these scrolls were stored in sealed jars and survived the ravages of time, so that many of them are readable today.

They are important because when they were found, they were one thousand years older than the previous earliest Old Testament manuscript. By comparing the manuscripts, we know that in one thousand years of copying, we have only one word in Isaiah 53, the word "light" in verse 11 as translated in the NIV, that is different from the previous earliest manuscript, and it affects the meaning of nothing. So for all practical purposes, we know that the Old Testament manuscript remained unchanged from one thousand years earlier. This gives us great confidence in the reliability of Bible manuscripts.

The copying of these manuscripts was done, in many cases, by dedicated, scholarly monks who viewed their task as a sacred labor of love. Some also believed that a curse fell on anyone who added or subtracted from the Scripture (Revelation 22:18–19). Therefore, exacting and painstaking measures were taken to ensure accuracy in the copying process. This is why variations in manuscripts are almost nonexistent, and this is why we believe that the Bible we have today is, for all practical purposes, exactly the same as was originally written.

Archaeological Evidence

Many of the attacks on the accuracy of the Bible were begun prior to modern archaeology. Beginning with major excavations in the Holy Land in the mid-1800s the Bible has been verified time and time again with archaeological evidence. As travel became easier, and scholars more curious, archaeologists began to peel away the earth's surface to reveal ancient cities, painted tombs, solid gold likenesses of rulers, jars, money and items needed for the afterlife, and tablets of stone and clay telling the story of a people or a city. As this evidence began to amass, references to biblical places and people became not unusual. In a number of cases, people or places that skeptics had written off as fanciful mistakes in the Bible were now confirmed. In fact, many things that were questioned by scholars in the eighteenth and nineteenth centuries have now been verified as factual, both cities and things in those cities, as well as rulers and important people.

For example, Belshazzar, named in the Book of Daniel as the last king of Babylon, was nowhere to be found in Babylonian records. In fact, all known Babylonian records listed Nabonidus as the last king. Then it was discovered in archaeological records that Nabonidus left Babylon for ten years and went to Arabia. His son, Belshazzar, ruled as king in his place. Nabonidus never abdicated his throne, but Belshazzar ruled as king in Babylon in his place during the time of Daniel. In this way, archaeology explained the apparent discrepancy between the biblical record and the previous Babylonian record.

Clifford Wilson, a retired archaeologist at the University of Sidney in Australia, and a committed Christian, has told of evidence of a man named Sanballat, found during the time of Alexander the Great. Yet, a man named Sanballat is also found in the Book of Nehemiah, before Alexander the Great's time. This was often cited by critics of the Bible as a historical error. But then it was discovered that there were three Sanballats, and that one of them lived during the time of Nehemiah, and the Bible was right after all.

More than a century of biblical excavations at over twenty-five thousand sites have repeatedly confirmed the accuracy of the Bible. After working in the field for many years, noted archaeologist Nelson Glueck said, "It may be stated categorically that no archaeological discovery has ever controverted (contradicted) a biblical reference" (*Evidence That Demands a Verdict*, Josh McDowell, 65).

Archaeology confirms the Bible's accuracy.

Now, to be completely candid, we must assess what all this means. This, by itself, does not mean that the Bible is the Word of God. All it means is that the Bible has never been proved to be wrong on any point of history or geography. However, that is one of the tests that must be passed if we are to conclude that the Bible is the Word of God. If there were mistakes in it, we would have trouble accepting it as the Word of God. Since there are no mistakes in it, it passes the historical/geographical test, and allows us, on that ground, to conclude that it could be the Word of God. Whether or not we decide it is the Word of God is ultimately a matter of faith, but we would have difficulty making that conclusion if we found the Bible riddled with error.

Fulfilled Prophecies

The Bible is the only book in the world that has specific prophecies made hundreds of years earlier that have been clearly fulfilled.

Prophecies in the Old Testament have been fulfilled referring to Jesus Christ; the nation of Israel; the nations of Babylonia, Persia, Greece, and Rome; cities such as Tyre and Babylon; and specific people such as Nebuchadnezzar and Cyrus. No other religious writing in the world has been fulfilled so completely and accurately as the Bible. In addition, prophecies in the New Testament concerning the life, death, and resurrection of Jesus, as well as prophecies concerning the early church, have been fulfilled exactly as they were written, while others have yet to be fulfilled. The number of prophecies that have been fulfilled are so numerous that statisticians calculating the odds of their being fulfilled by chance have concluded that it is impossible for them to be a coincidence.

HOW DOES THE BIBLE DESCRIBE
THE HUMAN CONDITION?

*The Bible accurately describes humanity as inherently
flawed and without ability to correct itself.*

To know the Bible well is to be in touch with reality—with the way things are. If you know the Bible, you know the thoughts, motives, and actions of humanity. For example, throughout modern history people have toyed with creating a utopia, but it has never worked. They have tried elaborate schemes to win voluntary participation in utopian behavior (such as the utopian society created in New Harmony, Indiana, over a hundred years ago). They have tried absolute force and domination (such as in the Soviet Union). They have tried small communal farms in central Tennessee, and they have tried New Age cults looking for redemption through extraterrestrial beings. But utopian societies always fail and always will fail. Why? Because humanity is fallen and cannot fulfill the ideals of a utopia. There will never be a man-made utopia on earth. The Bible teaches that while humanity is capable of doing good, it is also incapable of not doing bad. And that bad streak prevents utopia. The Bible is true to what is.

In another example, the Bible says, talking about sexual immorality, that "every other sin that a man commits is outside the body, but the immoral man sins against his own body" (1 Corinthians 6:18 NASB). And, when a society tolerates sexual immorality, inevitably sexually transmitted diseases become rampant. From syphilis to gonorrhea to herpes to AIDS, sexually transmitted diseases ravage the bodies of those who are sexually immoral. The immoral man does sin against his own body. The Bible is true to what is.

In a further example, the Bible says that the key to harmonious relationship is the principle of mutual submission (Ephesians 5:21). Whether it is husband/wife relationships, parent/child relationships, or employer/employee relationships, mutual submission is the key to harmony. In each relationship, the one in authority is submissive to the needs of those under his authority, and each one is submissive to the authority of the one over him. When this mutual submission is practiced, each person gets his needs met in a context of unity. When mutual submission is not practiced, needs are not met, and there is a context of strife and division. The Bible is true to what is. The Bible always accurately describes the human condition, which lends credibility to the Bible's reliability.

The Bible is true to what is.

HOW HAS THE BIBLE INFLUENCED HUMANITY?

The Bible has had a positive influence on humanity wherever it has been known and followed.

The Bible has had a major impact on the world. Wherever it has gone and been revered, the Bible has created progress for humanity and an improvement in the human condition. Regarding the family, the Bible says that husbands are to love their wives as Christ loved the church and gave Himself up for it, while wives are to respect their husbands. Parents are not to exasperate their children, but to bring them up in the training and admonition of the Lord, while children are to obey their parents in the Lord (Ephesians 5:22–6:9). Where these principles have been followed, marriages and families have flourished and provided the stability for a strong society.

Regarding labor, the Bible instructs those in authority to do their job as unto the Lord, while those in authority are to care for the needs of those under authority, knowing that the Master of them both is in heaven (Colossians 3:22–24). Where these principles have been followed, productivity has increased and economies have flourished.

Regarding race relations, the Bible flatly repudiates racial or any other kind of discrimination. Luke 6:31 says that we should do unto others as we would have others do unto us. If we would not be discriminated against, we should not discriminate. Period. All discrimination is sin. James, the brother of Jesus, wrote in the Bible, "If you show partiality [to people], you commit sin, and are convicted by the law as transgressors" (James 2:9). Therefore, where this teaching has been accepted, discrimination has disappeared. While the putting aside of discrimination may seem rare in the world, we might shudder to think how bad it might

The Bible has improved the human condition.

be if it were not for the influence of the Bible. It was Christians who led the fight against slavery, both in England and in the United States, and while discrimination still exists, that is in spite of what the Bible teaches, not because of it.

Regarding crime, the Bible says flatly, "You shall not steal" (Exodus 20:15). Where the Bible has been highly regarded, crime has diminished.

Humanitarianism (caring for the disadvantaged) has been spurred by the Bible wherever it has been held in high regard. Scripture teaches that to the degree we care for those who are unable to care for themselves, we serve Jesus (Matthew 25:31–46). History records very scant evidence of significant expressions of humanitarianism before the rise of Christianity. Today, hospitals and relief efforts throughout the world have been created by Christian organizations for humanitarian relief.

The Bible charges government to do good and serve the needs of humanity (Romans 13:3), while citizens are charged to respect those governments. Where these principles are obeyed, government serves the needs of the people, and the people are loyal to their government. When these principles are violated, government tyrannizes citizens and citizens rebel against government. Chaos and suffering reign. From the empire of Rome to Genghis Khan to Mussolini to Hitler to Stalin to Mao, a thousand tyrants have barbarously inflicted their godless will on millions of people. By contrast, the nations that have embraced the principle of Scripture have taken into account the needs of their citizens and have tried, within the obvious limitations of all political systems, to bring justice to their country.

Regarding education, a knowledge of the Scripture has been the driving force for literacy wherever the gospel has gone. Deuteronomy 6:6–7 says, "These words which I command you today shall be in your heart. You shall teach them diligently to your children." The urgent purpose to which the first printing press was put was the printing of Bibles. Since then, wherever the Bible has been held in high esteem, literacy has been prized. In the United States, all the early universities until the University of Pennsylvania, including Harvard, Yale, and Princeton, were founded initially for the training of clergy to teach the Scriptures to the new nation. In addition, missionary efforts around the world since the founding of those universities have focused on reducing languages to writing for the purpose of giving new languages the Bible in their tongue. Christianity has been perhaps the greatest force for literacy and education in the history of the world.

The Bible has also historically given us the greatest subjects and artists for art, music, and literature. Wherever these expressions of the soul of humanity have achieved their highest cultivation, the impact of the Bible has been unmistakable.

The Bible has affected the world to a more profound degree than most of us have the information to realize. Without the Bible, it would be a much different— and much deficient—world in which we live. If, when followed properly, the Bible has brought only benefit to humanity, it lends credibility to its spiritual message. These facts also support the reliability of the Bible.

CONCLUSION

When we see that the Bible has impacted our world in a major way, that it has been the subject for much of the greatest art and music ever created, that it has helped bring justice and compassion to the home, the workplace, and governments, when we consider that the original Bible manuscripts contained no errors of fact and that Bible prophecies have been fulfilled after hundreds and sometimes thousands of years, then it sets the stage for believing the Bible when it tells us what our spiritual condition is, when it tells us how we are to relate to God, when it tells us what our future is without Christ and what our future is with Christ.

If the Bible demonstrates itself to be credible in the physical realm, we have reason to believe it when it speaks of spiritual matters. In his book *Defending Your Faith*, Dan Story has written:

> The Bible is an historical document of demonstrated accuracy and reliability. In every area in which it can be checked-out—historically, culturally, geographically, scientifically, and so on—it has been verified as factual by extra-biblical sources. It is full of information on the history of the Jews and other ancient civilizations, as well as early Christianity. It presents unique and invaluable information on the customs, languages, cultures, ethics, and religion of what is the foundation of all Western civilization. Because of this, and in spite of the Bible's religious significance, . . . it should be used as a resource for historical information in public schools.
>
> [Further], if the Bible alone *can* sustain its truthful claims in areas in which it can be investigated, then it is reasonable to trust it in spiritual matters. We have a solid foundation from which to assert that what the Bible says about Jesus as Lord and Savior, sin and its consequences, and the path to salvation must be correct. And if what the Bible says is true, contrary religious claims must be false. (33–34)

SPEED BUMP!

Slow down to be sure you've gotten the main points from this chapter.

Q1. What claim does the Bible make for itself?

A1. The Bible claims to be the Word of God, without *error*.

Q2. Why do we believe the Bible is reliable?

A2. Ancient manuscripts, archaeology, and prophecy all *support* the reliability of the Bible.

Q3. How does the Bible describe the human condition?

A3. The Bible accurately describes humanity as inherently *flawed* and without ability to correct itself.

Q4. How has the Bible influenced humanity?

A4. The Bible has had a *positive* influence on humanity wherever it has been known and followed.

FILL IN THE BLANK

Q1. What claim does the Bible make for itself?

A1. The Bible claims to be the Word of God, without _____.

Q2. Why do we believe the Bible is reliable?

A2. Ancient manuscripts, archaeology, and prophecy all _____ the reliability of the Bible.

Q3. How does the Bible describe the human condition?

A3. The Bible accurately describes humanity as inherently _____ and without ability to correct itself.

Q4. How has the Bible influenced humanity?

A4. The Bible has had a _____ influence on humanity wherever it has been known and followed.

FOR FURTHER THOUGHT AND DISCUSSION

1. In what ways have you personally experienced or observed that the Bible is true to what is?

2. What positive influence has the Bible had on you that helps you believe it is true?

3. When you consider the accuracy of the Bible concerning past fulfilled prophecies, what do you think it suggests concerning presently unfulfilled prophecies?

WHAT IF I DON'T BELIEVE?

If I don't believe the Bible is true, I have no way to know anything for sure about God, about meaning in life, and about life after death. Without the Bible, we can only guess at reality and each person's guess is as good as the next. I am left without any way to know anything for sure. I am left without any reason for hope.

FOR FURTHER STUDY

1. Scripture

- 2 Timothy 3:16–17
- Hebrews 4:12

2. Books

Know Why You Believe, Paul Little
Defending Your Faith, Dan Story
Handbook of Christian Apologetics, Peter Kreeft and Ronald Tacelli

CHAPTER 5

HOW CAN WE SAY THAT JESUS IS THE ONLY WAY TO GOD?

A person may go to heaven without health, without riches, without honors, without learning, without friends; but he can never go there without Christ.
—John Dyer (1699–1757)

There are many roads up the mountain, but they all lead to the top," she said, using the well-known analogy to make the point that there may be many different religions, all sincerely worshiping the same God. This lady claimed to be a Christian, and she had spent most of her life in the church. She was trying to soften my conviction that Jesus was the only way to God.

This is a common perception today in our age of tolerance in which almost anything is tolerated except intolerance. And the ultimate intolerance, in many people's minds, is telling someone they will go to hell because they are worshiping the wrong God. To say, "I'm right and I'm going to heaven, but you're wrong and you're going to hell," is seen as the ultimate power trip.

Many people object to the Christian claim that Jesus is the only way to God. First, they believe, it fails to respect other religions; second, it fails to appreciate the value of sincerity (if someone sincerely worships the wrong god, surely the true God would excuse that, and assume that with the full information he would be worshiping the true God). People also say that it seems cruel and unfair to condemn the great masses of people who have died without ever hearing the name of Jesus. They don't believe a loving God would do such a thing.

People today claim there are many ways to God.

A number of "untouchable" doctrines of Christianity are being "touched" these days. In some cases, the untouchable doctrines are being touched by people whose runaway compassion moves them to adopt incorrect positions regardless of what the Scripture says. In other cases, they are being touched by responsible evangelical scholars who truly believe that the Bible demands a new look at some old beliefs.

A major one is the doctrine of hell. The traditional idea of a literal lake of fire is being questioned in favor of a more symbolic interpretation ("fire" equals "spiritual and emotional anguish," and so on). Another one is whether all those who have not heard and believed in the claims of Christ will be condemned to hell. These doctrines were challenged decades ago by liberals who rejected the idea that Scripture was divinely inspired and therefore accurate and authoritative in all things. The difference today is that the questions are being asked by scholars who accept the inspiration, accuracy, and authority of Scripture, but they believe we may have misinterpreted the teachings of Scripture on these and other historical doctrines.

IN THIS CHAPTER WE LEARN THAT . . .

1. We can say Jesus is the only way to God because the Bible says He is the only way.
2. The Christian community is increasingly divided on whether or not a person can be saved without having heard of Jesus.
3. There is a general consensus that those who cannot understand the gospel will be saved.

In this chapter we want to explore the vital doctrine that Jesus is the only way. How can we make such a claim? Is there any possible way for people to be saved if they have never heard of the name of Jesus?

WHY WOULD ANYONE SAY THAT JESUS IS THE ONLY WAY TO GOD?

We can say Jesus is the only way to God because the Bible says He is the only way.

Dan Story, in his book *Defending Your Faith*, wrote about encountering a lady who epitomized many people's perspective of Jesus and Christianity:

Just before Easter Sunday, I had the opportunity to share with a lady who claimed to have had a profound religious experience. She was once a Christian, but this other incident had totally transformed her life. She did not clearly state what her religious experience entailed, but it resulted in a firm belief that her personal encounter with deity was a genuine revelation. Moreover, she was convinced that Jesus was just a man who achieved "Christhood" through His own spiritual enlightenment (in a way, I suppose, similar to her own), and that Satan was a myth. She considered Jesus one of the many prophets and the Bible one of many holy books. The writings of Buddha, Confucius, Mohammed, Moses, and others were all divine revelations that ultimately lead faithful searches to the same God.

As our conversation progressed, it became apparent that she had never considered Christianity in light of its historical evidences. Rather, its truth-claims rested solely on one's subjective opinions. Thus it merited no more or no less consideration than any other religion, allowing her to decide in her own mind its authenticity. She is not alone in this view.

Many non-Christians assume that all religions are paths to the same mountaintop, that all religions lead to the Supreme Being and eternal bliss. The implication is that all religions are equal. (109–110)

Christians are accused of being narrow-minded when they claim that Jesus is the only means of salvation. However, Christians did not invent the idea just to be unpopular. Neither do they believe it because they want to be right when everyone else is wrong. Rather, it is part of Christian teaching because the Bible itself makes the claim, and Christians are trying to be true to the Bible.

Jesus said, "I am the way, the truth, and the life. No one comes to the Father except through Me" (John 14:6), and, "If you do not believe that I am [the Savior], you will die in your sins" (John 8:24). The apostle Peter said, "Nor is there salvation in any other, for there is no other name under heaven given among men by which we must be saved" (Acts 4:12). The apostle Paul wrote, "For there is one God and one Mediator between God and men, the Man Christ Jesus" (1 Timothy 2:5). These statements

Jesus is the way of salvation.

are straightforward, and all agree with each other. No one can get to God the Father without coming through Jesus. Jesus is the only way of salvation.

But why would God make this the requirement? It is because of who He is and who we are. He is holy and perfect, and He created humanity in His image. God fellowshipped without interference with Adam and Eve in the Garden of Eden. But then Adam and Eve sinned against God, eating from the Tree of the Knowledge of

Good and Evil, from which they had been forbidden to eat. They were warned that if they broke this commandment they would die (Genesis 2:7).

Four areas of devastation resulted from their sin. First, Adam and Eve were cut off from God (Genesis 3:8). Second, relationships with other humans were broken (Genesis 3:12–13). Third, the easy relationship between humanity and nature was broken (Genesis 3:17–18). Finally, each individual became alienated from himself and riddled with loneliness, lack of meaning, purposelessness, and an inability to love others consistently.

Sin separates us from God.

The consequence of all this is a hard life on earth and eternal separation from God. But God loved us. He provided a way for us to be restored to Him and potentially restored to each other, to nature, and to ourselves. He sent a Savior to die for our sins and allow us to be made new and reconciled to God. This way was Jesus. Jesus died in our place in order that we could be restored to God. "God was in Christ reconciling the world to Himself," and "He made Him who knew no sin to be sin for us, that we might become the righteousness of God in Him" (2 Corinthians 5:19, 21).

Jesus did for us what we could not do for ourselves. Someone has said, "He became what we were so we could become what He is." That's stretching it a bit, because we will never become the infinite God, but Scripture says that in some capacity, "we shall be like Him, for we shall see Him as He is" (1 John 3:2).

It is sin, and sin alone, that separates us from God. And sin must be dealt with God's way in order for us to be reconciled to God. Being reconciled to God is not a matter of goodness (our being good enough). It is a matter of perfection (we must be perfect, not just good). That is why we need a savior. That is why we need our sins to be atoned, paid for. Jesus was the only one who could do it. He was both God and man. If He were not man, He could not have died in our place for our sins. If He were not God, it would not have mattered if He had. He is the only way we can be reconciled to God. This whole theme is dealt with more extensively in another volume in this series, *What You Need to Know about Salvation*.

Josh McDowell, in his book *Answers to Tough Questions*, posed the following scenario:

Suppose a group of us are taking a hike in a very dense forest. As we get deeper into the forest, we become lost.

Realizing that taking the wrong path now might mean we will lose our lives, we begin to be afraid. However, we soon notice that ahead in the distance where the trail splits, there are two human forms at the fork in the road.

Running up to these people, we notice that one has on a park ranger uniform, and he is standing there perfectly healthy and alive, while the other person is lying face down, dead. Now which of these two are we going to ask about the way out? Obviously, the one who is living.

When it comes to eternal matters, we are going to ask the one who is alive the way out of the predicament. This is not Mohammed, not Confucius, but Jesus Christ. Jesus is unique. He came back from the dead. This demonstrates He is the one whom He claimed to be (Romans 1:4), the unique Son of God and the only way by which a person can have a personal relationship with the true and living God. (63–64)

Christians say Jesus is the only way to God because the Bible says He is, and because we believe He has risen from the dead to validate His claims. Virtually everyone agrees that Mohammed is dead, that Confucius is dead, that Siddhartha Gautama is dead. Jesus is the only one who claims to be God, the only one who claims to be able to forgive sin, and the only one who claims to have risen from the dead. If it is all true, then why wouldn't we believe Jesus is the only way to God?

CAN PEOPLE BE SAVED WHO HAVE NEVER HEARD OF JESUS?

The Christian community is increasingly divided on whether or not a person can be saved without having heard of Jesus.

The traditional teaching of Christianity has been that all those who die without hearing the name of Christ and without having an opportunity to respond specifically to the message of salvation in Him are eternally separated from God. This understanding is based on the passages we have already looked at, which demonstrate that salvation can be experienced only through Jesus: John 14:6; Acts 4:12; and 1 John 5:11–12. It is often called the "exclusive" position or the "restrictive" position, because it excludes or restricts from salvation those who have never believed in Jesus. Ancient theologians such as Saint Augustine, a bishop in the early church; John Calvin, a leader of the Protestant Reformation; and Jonathan Edwards, a leading early American preacher and theologian, have skillfully articulated this position. It is also advanced by modern American theologians such as Carl F. H. Henry and R. C. Sproul.

God treats everyone justly.

However, this position is being rethought by some evangelicals today, for theological and biblical reasons. These include a belief that the love of God is wider and more inclusive than commonly or previously thought. In John 12:32, Jesus said,

"And I, if I am lifted up from the earth [crucified], will draw all peoples to Myself." The apostle Peter stated that the Lord is "patient . . . not wishing for any to perish but for all to come to repentance" (2 Peter 3:9 NASB). The apostle Paul wrote that God our Savior "desires all men to be saved and to come to the knowledge of the truth" (1 Timothy 2:4). From these passages we see that God wants everyone to be saved.

In addition, God will treat everyone justly. Throughout the Scripture, we see the righteousness and justice of God upheld in His dealings with all people (Genesis 18:25; Psalm 145:17). So if God will deal justly with all people, and if He wants all people to be saved, what do we say about the millions of people who have lived and died without ever having heard the name of Jesus? "Inclusivism" teaches that those who have never heard the name of Jesus may be saved if they respond to God in faith based on the revelation they have. What kind of God, they ask, would make enough of Himself known to make persons guilty for rejecting Him, but not enough for their salvation?

Nature

The idea of "general revelation," which refers to the limited information that can be known about God through nature and inner conscience, is very important to this inclusive position. John 1:9 says that there is a light that "gives light to every man coming into the world." But how does every person coming into the world receive light? The apostle Paul tells us one way in Romans 1:19–20:

> What may be known of God is manifest in [unbelievers], for God has shown it to them. For since the creation of the world His invisible attributes are clearly seen, being understood by the things that are made, even His eternal power and Godhead, so that they are without excuse.

From this passage we learn that God has shown to everyone His essential nature through the created world. When we look at the starry heavens, when we ponder nature around us, we have enough information to conclude that a God of eternal power exists. David shared his experience of the wonder of God when he wrote Psalm 19:1–6.

God is revealed through nature and conscience.

Paul's speech to the people of the ancient city of Lystra included additional information about general revelation. In that speech, Paul stated that God gave a witness of Himself to the world through His providential blessings on all people. "[God] did not leave Himself without witness, in that He did good, gave us rain from heaven and fruitful seasons, filling our hearts with food and gladness" (Acts 14:17).

Conscience

In addition to the general revelation of nature, God has revealed Himself through the human conscience. In Romans 1, after stating that something could be known of God through nature, Paul said that unbelievers who have no written record of God's laws still have in their consciences some understanding of God's moral demands. Speaking of a long list of sins (murder, envy, strife, deceit), Paul said of the wicked people who do these things that, though they know God's decrees—that those who do such things deserve to die—they not only do them but approve of those who practice them (verses 29–32).

People who reject God are without excuse.

Paul then talked about the role of the conscience in Gentiles who do not have the written law of God:

> When Gentiles, who do not have the law, by nature do the things [contained] in the law, these, although not having the law, are a law to themselves, who show the work of the law written in their hearts, their conscience also bearing witness. (Romans 2:14–15)

While people may have an intuitive sense that God exists, sometimes this knowledge is distorted or suppressed (Romans 1:18). The knowledge of who God is, and the knowledge of His moral law, is never perfect, but it is enough to give an awareness of God's demands on humanity. He is a good God who does what is right, and He expects people to do what is right. Even if their concept of right and wrong is not completely biblical, it is still enough to demonstrate that all people violate even their own standards of morality and are therefore guilty according to their own standards, let alone God's.

Perhaps this inner witness of conscience is what Solomon was alluding to when he said, "[God] has put eternity in their hearts" (Ecclesiastes 3:11). The knowledge of God's existence, character, and moral law comes to all humanity through creation and conscience, so that all who reject God are without excuse.

If, however, people believe that there is a God because of what they see of Him in nature, and if they believe that they should therefore try to live a good life in honor of this God, then the inclusivists say these people are responding in faith to what they know of God. Therefore, if they were to hear of the gospel of salvation by grace through faith in Jesus, they would accept it because to truly accept God is to also truly accept Jesus. Because of this essential faith in God, responding as fully as their information allows them to respond, God accepts their faith and imputes it to them as righteousness.

Inclusivists place a number of qualifications on general revelation. First, they admit that it is inferior to specific revelation (i.e., Scripture). Second, the knowledge gained through general revelation is not merely the result of human reasoning, but also through the illumining ministry of God (Romans 1:19). Third, they emphasize that no one is saved by his own reasoning or efforts; no one is saved by good works, but by the grace of God. Finally, they do not deny the universal sinfulness of humanity. The benefit of general revelation, then, is that God has regard for the faith a person places in Him even when the faith is incomplete.

Hebrews 11:6 says that God is a rewarder of those who diligently seek Him. Just as Abraham, Melchizedek, Jethro, and Job in the Old Testament came to a saving knowledge of God apparently without Scripture and without a specific knowledge of Jesus, so can those today who have never heard. Many people today are spiritually "before Christ" as these men were, even though they are chronologically "after Christ." Just as Jews lived before Christ on the basis of redemption yet to be revealed to them, so are those today who have never heard of Jesus, who in their hearts have responded as fully to the God of nature and conscience as they know how. According to the inclusivists, the person is still saved by Jesus, because it is only as a result of the substitutionary atonement of Christ that the person's faith could be counted as righteousness.

WHY I NEED TO KNOW THIS

I need to know this so that I can defend my faith against those who would distort it and deny it on false grounds.

Ancient adherents to this position include Justin Martyr and John Wesley; modern proponents include the well-known authors and scholars C. S. Lewis, Clark Pinnock, and Peter Kreeft.

Exclusivists generally fall into two camps. One camp suggests that all who will be saved are predestined to salvation, and that if someone dies without the opportunity to hear of Christ he was not predestined to salvation. Others declare that if a person responds genuinely in his heart to the general revelation available to him, to the extent that God sees he would accept Jesus if given the chance, then God will see to it that that person will hear of Jesus.

I will never forget, shortly after becoming a Christian, hearing the story of a missionary who made a heroic effort to reach a remote tribe in the headwaters of the Amazon River. He traveled by canoe for many days up a tributary to reach this unreached tribe. In his canoe were the provisions he would need for his stay, as well as some Portuguese Bibles. Before he reached his destination, his canoe capsized, his provisions were lost, and he contracted a serious fever. He barely made it back to civilization with his life. It was nearly a year before he regained enough health to repeat the trip.

When he got to his destination and learned enough of the language to tell the people about Jesus, they responded that they already knew of Him and worshiped Him. The missionary was astounded. How could it be? Then the story unfolded. Before the missionary had made his first trip, a man from the tribe left and migrated to a city where he found employment and learned the Portuguese language. He soon became disillusioned with modern life, however,

> **In Christ, one's faith is counted as righteousness.**

and eventually returned to his homeland. On his trip back, he was paddling up the river when he spotted a book by the edge of the river. It was a Portuguese Bible that had been lost from the missionary's first trip. He took the Bible home, read it, and told his people what he was reading. The entire tribe came to know Christ.

Exclusivists use a story like this to demonstrate the lengths to which God will go to get the gospel to those who will believe. God is able to get His message to receptive hearts.

Inclusivists object, however, and state that such stories, while true, do not account for the vast majority of humanity who never have any contact with the gospel. What about the centuries that passed without any of the multiplied millions in Mongolia hearing about Jesus? The sheer weight of the numbers of people involved make the exclusivist position unacceptable, they say, because surely in all those years God somehow would have brought at least a few Mongolians to hear and respond in faith in Jesus.

WHAT ABOUT THOSE WHO CANNOT UNDERSTAND THE GOSPEL?

There is a general consensus that those who cannot understand the gospel will be saved.

On the heels of the question about what happens to those who have never heard the gospel, people often wonder about those who cannot understand it, such as infants and those with severe mental disabilities. The agreement on this issue is not absolute. For example, one position is that God elects those who will be saved, and if someone cannot understand the gospel, he will go to heaven if he is elect and to hell if he is not.

Others do not see it as cut and dried. It is commonly held, on the basis of 2 Samuel 12:23, that infants who are too young to understand the gospel will go to heaven. In this passage, David is mourning the death of his newborn son, and he says, "I will go to him, but he will not return to me" (NASB). This is often quoted at funerals of infants for the comfort it brings to grieving family members. Others believe that the passage is merely about death; that is, David was saying, "I will die as my son has died. He will not come back to life again."

Other passages dealing with children include Matthew 19:14–15, Mark 10:13–16, and Luke 18:16–17, which are parallel passages about children who are brought to Jesus. The disciples tried to stop people from bringing the children, but Jesus said, "Let the little children come to Me, and do not forbid them; for of such is the kingdom of heaven." The suggestion by some is that all children are members of the kingdom of heaven. Others believe that Jesus was saying that, in order to enter the kingdom of heaven, adults need faith in God like little children have in their parents.

Another position is more complicated, but it results in the belief that all children and mentally handicapped people who are incapable of understanding the gospel are saved. It suggests that, while only the elect are saved, God would not send anyone to judgment unless that person understood why. Adults who reject Jesus, even those who have not heard of Him, will know why they are in hell when they get there—they will understand that they rejected what they knew of God through nature and conscience. But those who cannot understand the gospel would not understand why they were in hell. Therefore, all who die before they can understand the gospel are elect (*How Shall They Be Saved*, Millard Erickson, 245–247).

Only the elect are saved.

While the agreement is not universal, there is a general consensus among Christians that those who die without being able to understand the gospel are saved.

CONCLUSION

The debate over whether someone can be saved without having heard the name of Jesus is sparking heated debate among Christian scholars. Those who believe that all who have not heard of Jesus are lost sometimes question the integrity of those who believe otherwise. They sometimes challenge the motives, the scholarship, and even the salvation of anyone who would toy with such a crucial doctrine. Some admit that the Bible is not absolutely clear on the issue, but that we should teach the "safest" interpretation—namely, that we should assume they are all lost so that missionary zeal is not diminished.

Those, on the other hand, who favor an inclusive approach believe that we should not strive for the safest position but for the position most accurate to Scripture and most consistent with the loving character of God. They claim that many people are turned away from Christianity because they cannot bring themselves to worship a God who would be so cold-hearted (in their understanding) as to eternally condemn someone who had never heard the way to be saved. In addition, they claim that missionary zeal need not be diminished because the gospel is indisputably furthered when the name of Christ is taken to those who have not heard. Only disobedient and hard-hearted people would refuse to carry the name of Jesus to every person possible.

> **God's character is always intact.**

Regardless of the final destiny of those who have never heard of Jesus, both sides would agree that when we know and understand the truth we will admit that God's perfect character is intact, and that the fate of the ignorant will be decided by a righteous God. No fault will be found in His ultimate decision for these people. Both sides must admit that whichever position is true, it does not change the commands in Scripture for Christlikeness on our part, nor does it remove Christ's charge to us to "go . . . make disciples of all the nations" (Matthew 28:19).

SPEED BUMP!

Slow down to be sure you've gotten the main points from this chapter.

Q1. Why would anyone say that Jesus is the only way to God?

A1. We can say Jesus is the only way to God because the *Bible* says He is the only way.

Q2. Can people who have never heard of Jesus be saved?

A2. The Christian community is increasingly *divided* on whether or not a person can be saved without having heard of Jesus.

Q3. What about those who cannot understand the gospel?

A3. There is a general *consensus* that those who cannot understand the gospel will be saved.

FILL IN THE BLANK

Q1. Why would anyone say that Jesus is the only way to God?

A1. We can say Jesus is the only way to God because the _____ says He is the only way.

Q2. Can people who have never heard of Jesus be saved?

A2. The Christian community is increasingly _____ on whether or not a person can be saved without having heard of Jesus.

Q3. What about those who cannot understand the gospel?

A3. There is a general _____ that those who cannot understand the gospel will be saved.

FOR FURTHER THOUGHT AND DISCUSSION

1. Does it disturb you that evangelical scholars are discussing the issue of whether anyone can be saved who has never heard of Jesus? Why or why not?

2. What do you believe about the issue? What information seems most persuasive to you?

3. What do you believe about the salvation of those who cannot understand the gospel? What information seems most persuasive to you?

WHAT IF I DON'T BELIEVE?

Regardless of what I believe on these issues, I must fully embrace the reality that none of the commands in the Bible regarding my character or behavior change. I am to still dedicate myself to manifesting the character and proclaiming the name of Christ as far as He calls and enables me to.

FOR FURTHER STUDY

1. Scripture

- Ecclesiastes 3:11
- John 12:32
- John 14:6
- Acts 4:12
- Romans 1:18–21
- Romans 2:14–15
- 2 Corinthians 5:19–21
- 1 Timothy 2:4–5
- 2 Peter 3:9

2. Books

How Shall They Be Saved? Millard Erickson
What About Those Who Have Never Heard? John Sanders (Ed.)
Four Views on Salvation in a Pluralistic World, Dennis L. Okholm and Timothy R. Phillips

CHAPTER **6**

I do not fear the explosive power of the atom bomb. What I fear is the explosive power of evil in the human heart.
—**Albert Einstein**

HOW DO WE RESOLVE THE PROBLEM OF EVIL?

The problem of evil, and the suffering it brings, is staggering. Hitler is considered by some the most evil person who ever lived. He was a racist who wanted to exterminate all those he considered inferior—that is, those who did not contribute to the advancement of his super-race. To him, they were merely human bacteria. He killed Jews, Christians, Gypsies, Slavs, Poles, and others he considered racially inferior.

His strategy was to work the condemned ones until they could no longer work or died. When they no longer contributed to the higher good, they were exterminated. Bullets were expensive, so the Nazis used poison gas on them. However, even the gas was used sparingly to economize, so that some of the victims were still alive when they were put into the ovens to be incinerated.

The first victims were insane and incurable people. Before long, the campaign broadened to include anyone the Nazis considered undesirable. In the end, six million Jews and perhaps as many as ten million others, many of them Christians, were exterminated.

However, Hitler may not be the most evil person who ever lived. In terms of numbers of people who suffered at his hands, he is dwarfed by others. Before him, Joseph Stalin, the father of modern communism, showed no mercy in his bid for power in the Russian revolution. It is commonly believed that Stalin killed as many as forty million of his own countrymen.

But Hitler and Stalin together do not match the record of Chairman Mao of China. Millions were killed in the revolution, and additional millions were killed later in the effort to "collectivize" the nation under the Communist system. Still more millions were killed in the later cultural revolution. It is thought that as many as 72 million died at the direction of Chairman Mao.

IN THIS CHAPTER WE LEARN THAT . . .

1. Evil originated with Satan and entered the world with Adam and Eve.

2. God cannot destroy all evil without destroying humanity.

3. An infinite, holy God has thoughts and ways that are higher than ours.

4. Evil and suffering are not good, but God can use them for good.

In addition to armed revolution, there are the evils of crime, domestic abuse, discrimination, famine, epidemics, earthquakes, floods, and other natural disasters. The amount of evil and suffering in the world is profound, mind-numbing. If one thinks about it on the individual level, for there is the real tragedy—one life at a time—the sensitive soul cannot take it in.

This has become a significant problem for Christianity in the eyes of many. They believe that the suffering in the world is incompatible with an all-good, all-powerful God. Therefore, a book on defending your faith must include a section dealing with suffering and the God of the Bible.

WHERE DID EVIL COME FROM?

Evil originated with Satan and entered the world with Adam and Eve.

The first account we have in the Bible of sin is with the fall of Lucifer, a high angel of God, who rebelled against God (Isaiah 14:12–15). All the Bible tells us about the origin of sin is that Lucifer was "perfect in your ways from the day you were created, *till iniquity was found in you*" (Ezekiel 28:15, emphasis added). All we know is that one day, iniquity was found in him. We can be no more specific than that. To say more than that is to say more than the Bible says. However, it is clear that the Bible does not blame God for iniquity. Lucifer carries his own blame.

Then, when God created the world, He pronounced it *very good* (Genesis 1:31). There was no evil or suffering on earth. When God created Adam and Eve, there was only one thing they were not permitted to do. They could not eat from the Tree of the Knowledge of Good and Evil. God warned them of the consequences, that if they disobeyed they would die. God gave them the freedom to choose to obey or disobey Him. Satan came to them in the form of a serpent; he tempted them, and they disobeyed. This was the way sin entered the world and the human race. Adam and Eve died spiritually with that sin, and the earth was transformed from a paradise to a place fraught with evil and suffering.

The fallen nature of Adam and Eve is passed down to all offspring, so that all of us are fallen. That is, we have a flawed nature in which we are not able to keep from sinning. We are not sinners because we sinned. Rather, we sin because we are born sinners (Romans 5:12–19). We commit *acts* of sin because we have a *nature* to sin.

> ## WHY I NEED TO KNOW THIS
>
> I need to know this so that I can have confidence in the goodness and power of God, and so that I will not be in danger of losing my faith because I accept the reasoning of the world on this issue.

Again, the Bible does not blame God for the sin. Adam and Eve are held accountable for their sin. We may protest that they were overwhelmed by the circumstances, and that God is responsible for the circumstances. We may protest that God knew it was going to happen and didn't head it off (He could easily have reappeared to Adam and Eve at the moment of temptation and brought them back to their senses). We may protest that we should not be held accountable for what someone else did. But no amount of objection changes the biblical record. Nowhere is God blamed for the existence of sin. Sin is said to have been found in Satan (Lucifer), who deceived Adam and Eve, who sinned. And as father and mother of the entire human race, they passed their fallen nature down to all of us. Both Satan and all humanity are held accountable to God for their sin.

WHY DOESN'T GOD REMOVE EVIL?

God cannot destroy all evil without destroying humanity.

God created humanity with an ability to choose. Not to have done so would have been to create robots. He loves us of His own free will, and He wants us to love Him of our own free will. Having the freedom to choose includes the possibility of choosing wrongly. And that's what we did. Concerning our free will, C. S. Lewis wrote, "The sin, both of men and of angels, was rendered possible by the fact that God gave them free will."

Each of us is contaminated by evil. Even Christians sin. God could not eliminate all evil without eliminating all of us. Most of the evil in the world is moral evil. Perhaps we could all agree that God should eliminate Adolf Hitler, but how about

Uncle Al who was a nice guy when sober, but when he was drunk, he beat his wife and abused his kids? Does God eliminate him? Perhaps you think so, but your sister doesn't. She thinks he deserves another chance. So does God take a vote of your family members? No matter what God would do in that situation, some people would think He was just by eliminating the evil, and others wouldn't.

> **Free will includes freedom to choose wrongly.**

As long as we have free will, there will be moral evil. Take away free will and you reduce humanity to a collection of fleshy automatons. Is there anyone reading this who would like to be stripped of his ability to choose? All meaning in life is dependent on that ability.

If God cannot destroy all evil without destroying humanity, and if that is too great a price to pay, then how do we deal with the presence of evil and suffering? There are several key issues that need to be addressed in dealing with the "fact" of evil and suffering.

C. S. Lewis stated it succinctly in his important work on this subject, *The Problem of Pain*:

> "If God were good, He would wish to make His creatures perfectly happy, and if God were almighty He would be able to do what He wished. But the creatures are not happy. Therefore God lacks either goodness, or power, or both." This is the problem of pain in its simplest form. (14)

However, Lewis did not accept the assumptions of God's critics. He said, with his typical insight, that we must clarify what is meant by the terms "almighty" and "goodness." Too often, critics champion a slogan that appears to take the moral and intellectual high ground, but which, on closer inspection, is fatally flawed.

What is meant by being almighty (omnipotent)? Lewis argued that it does not mean that God can do everything or anything. Rather, because of God's character and the nature of truth, once God has chosen to do one thing, it might make it impossible for Him to do the opposite.

> If you choose to say "God can give a creature free-will and at the same time withhold free-will from it," you have not succeeded in saying *anything* about God: meaningless combinations of words do not suddenly acquire a meaning because we prefix to them the two other words: "God can." It remains true that all *things* are possible with God: the intrinsic impossibilities are not things but nonentities. It is no more possible for God than for the weakest of His creatures to carry out both of two mutually exclusive alternatives, not because His power meets an obstacle, but because nonsense remains nonsense, even when we talk it about God. (16)

God cannot, for example, create a round square, or dark light, or dry water, because all that is nonsense. It is inherent contradiction, and God is not the author of nonsense or contradiction. It is inconsistent with His character.

Suffering cannot be a result of a lack of divine power. If God has created the universe, and then gives humanity free will, then suffering is certain to follow. So, just as God cannot create a round circle, He cannot create a world in which His creatures have freedom of choice and also have a world free from suffering. Lewis asserted, "Try to exclude the possibility of suffering which the order of nature and the existence of free-wills involve, and you will find that you have excluded life itself" (22).

As Lewis continued in *The Problem of Pain*, he challenged the common perception of "goodness." Goodness is the natural outcome and expression of the love of God. So the question is, "Is suffering inconsistent with a loving God?" Lewis insisted that we avoid a trivial and sentimental understanding of love. The love of God, Lewis argued,

> is not a senile benevolence that drowsily wishes you to be happy in your own way, nor the cold philanthropy of a conscientious magistrate, nor the care of a host who feels himself responsible for the comfort of his guests, but the consuming fire itself, the love that made the worlds, persistent as the artist's love for his work and despotic as a man's love for a dog, provident and venerable as a father's love for a child, jealous, inexorable, exacting as love between the sexes. (35)

The love of God is not some happy-go-lucky characteristic designed to put a constant smile on our face, a perpetual whistle on our lips, and a lilt to our every step. "The problem of reconciling human suffering with the existence of a God who loves is only insoluble so long as we attach a trivial meaning to the word 'love'" (*The Problem of Pain* 36).

In addition, the Bible resolutely declares that God is good, and that His works are good, and that God causes all things to work together for good to those who love Him (Romans 8:28). We must affirm the goodness of God or else rip pages and pages from our Bible. Of course there are many who would gladly do so, but others would be reluctant, and for those people, this point is important.

HOW CAN GOD BE GOOD AND STILL ALLOW EVIL AND SUFFERING?

An infinite, holy God has thoughts and ways that are higher than ours.

Certainly, we cannot simply look the other way and say that God is good, no matter what He does. We could not say that God is good if there were no evidence to support it. But the Bible says that God is good. The Bible is full of the good works of God. God has provided a way for humanity to be saved from its sin. God Himself came to earth, was born as Jesus of Nazareth, and died for our sins so that we would not have to. He paid our price for us.

Whatever the mystery behind the existence of sin, there is sufficient evidence to uphold the goodness of God. Had He stayed in heaven, leaving us to grovel in our own pain and find our own way to heaven, if possible, we might have a case against God. But because He came and entered our condition—became sin for us, that we might become the righteousness of God (2 Corinthians 5:21)—there is reason to believe that God is good. John Newton, author of the hymn "Amazing Grace," once said, "Many have puzzled themselves about the origin of evil. I am content to observe that there is evil, and that there is a way to escape from it, and with this I begin and end." Some might consider that statement insufficient explanation, but it carries a valid point. If God claims He is not the author of evil, and if He sent His Son to die for us to give us a way to escape the eternal consequences of evil, is there not sufficient evidence to vindicate the character of God?

Sometimes we don't understand because we don't have all the information.

When we try to make sense out of suffering, we can, I believe, safely assume that there is some information we don't have. Why God created when He knew sin would enter His creation, we may not know. There are many things about God that we are too small to carry. We just don't have all the information, or we don't have the ability to understand.

Finally, we must see things from God's point of view. He is not out to get us, nor is He out to neglect us. He is out to make us like Him, and for reasons hidden deep in the mysteries of His will, He allows and uses pain.

God is not out to get us.

However, God is not unaware or unaffected by our suffering. He does not leave us to suffer alone. He is not regaling the departed saints in a celestial party, oblivious to our plight, waiting for the day when we will finally join them. Rather, God is with us, always. When we hurt, God hurts. He feels our pain. In some mysterious way, this God who is complete and lacks nothing still links Himself with our suffering.

When it comes to God's identifying with our suffering, I have always felt that Jesus had credibility because He came to earth and suffered for me. So when He asks me to suffer, while I may not enjoy it, He has credibility with me. The Bible teaches that Jesus delighted to do the Father's will, but He did not delight to go to the cross. Scripture says that Jesus "endured the cross" (Hebrews 12:2). Luke 22:44 indicates that in the Garden of Gethsemane, Jesus was in emotional agony, and sweat profusely. Hebrews 5:7 says He cried. He asked for the help of friends who deserted Him in Mark 14:32. So if Jesus asks anything of me, I feel a sense of fraternity with Him. Anything He asks me to suffer will be less than He suffered for me.

But I confess to struggling with God the Father. It always seemed unfair to me for God to be up in His celestial glory, untouched by the ravages of sin in the world, telling me to be patient, that it would all be over some day, and we'd get our reward.

However, as I searched the Scriptures, I discovered how wrong I was. God feels our pain. He takes it into His own heart. When we hurt, God hurts. Not only does He feel pain for us, but for all those on earth; and not only all those on earth, but all those who have ever been on earth, and all those who will be on earth. Those of you who are parents know how much pain you go through watching your children hurt. When they are in physical or emotional pain, your heart breaks with them. In the same way, God hurts when He sees us hurting.

> **When we hurt, God hurts.**

Scripture says, "God was in Christ reconciling the world to Himself" (2 Corinthians 5:19). Where is God when it hurts? He is on the cross, taking to Himself in Christ the pain, agony, and terror of all the suffering of all the world for all time. We are united with Christ. When we suffer, God the Father suffers. When we are in pain, God feels and hears and cares.

It is as Dorothy Sayers wrote:

> For whatever reason God chose to make man as he is—limited and suffering and subject to sorrows and death—He had the honesty and courage to take His own medicine. Whatever game He is playing with His creation, He has kept His own rules and played fair. He can exact nothing from man that He has not exacted from Himself. He has Himself gone through the whole of human experience, from the trivial irritations of family life and the cramping restrictions of hard work and lack of money to the worst horrors of pain and humiliation, defeat, despair, and death. When He was a man, He played the man. He was born in poverty and died in disgrace and thought it well worthwhile. (quoted in *Open Windows* by Philip Yancey, 164)

No, God does not escape. He has chosen not to escape. Even from heaven, when I hurt, God hurts. Therefore, there must be a reason for the suffering that lies beyond my knowledge or understanding.

WHAT GOOD CAN COME OF EVIL AND SUFFERING?

Evil and suffering are not good, but God can use them for good.

There are a number of ways that God can use suffering in our lives. While these reasons do not justify the existence of pain, they reveal the good to which suffering can be used by the grace of God.

Prevention of Greater Pain

While evil and suffering are not good in themselves, they can be used for good. In a fallen world, pain can be a gift to turn us from an action so that we do not experience even greater pain. For example, if we touch our finger to a hot stove, we pull back in pain with a small burn that has kept us from a large, damaging, or life-threatening burn. The same is true of emotional pain. If we feel guilty because of a petty theft of a candy bar, the emotional pain may keep us from greater thefts that could be life-destroying.

Giving Spiritual Enlightenment

Pain can also be used for spiritual purposes. For example, in 2 Corinthians 1:1–11 we read three good things that God can bring out of suffering. First is that we can learn to comfort others.

> Blessed be the God and Father of our Lord Jesus Christ, the Father of mercies and God of all comfort, who comforts us in all our tribulation, that we may be able to comfort those who are in any trouble, with the comfort with which we ourselves are comforted by God. (verses 3–4)

Anyone who has gone through a heartbreak, a time of loneliness, or a period of great pain and has been comforted by God is able to comfort those who go through a similar trial. There is a mutual understanding, a credibility, a kindredness of spirit that makes one better able to help the other. Because of this, our suffering is never in vain, since there will always be others who have suffered as we have.

A second thing we learn is to trust not in ourselves but in God who can see us through our difficulties. In verses 8–9 we read that the apostle Paul was "burdened beyond measure, above strength, . . . that we should not trust in ourselves but in God who raises the dead."

It seems that we are often inclined to try to go through life in our strength as long as we can, and often never learn the lesson of dependency on God until we are forced to—until we are taken beyond our ability to cope and learn that we need God's strength.

Third, we can learn to give thanks in all things because of God's mercy and grace. In verse 11 Paul added, "you also helping together in prayer for us, that thanks may be given by many persons on our behalf for the gift granted to us through many." The apostle Paul thanked the Corinthian believers for praying for him when he was in such difficulty. In our trials and pain, we learn that we need God and we need others, and can be thankful when we experience how important they all are to our lives.

Creating Spiritual Growth

There are times when God uses discipline in the lives of His spiritual children for their good. The writer of the Book of Hebrews tells us that there are benefits we can experience through suffering. First, we can receive encouragement because discipline assures us that we are, in fact, children of God:

> My son, do not despise the chastening of the LORD, nor be discouraged when you are rebuked by Him; for whom the LORD loves He chastens, and scourges every son whom He receives. (Hebrews 12:5–6)

Second, God disciplines us because, through discipline, we can share in God's holiness and reap the reward of righteousness:

> He [disciplines] for our profit, that we may be partakers of His holiness. Now no chastening seems to be joyful for the present, but painful; nevertheless, afterward it yields the peaceable fruit of righteousness to those who have been trained by it. (Hebrews 12:10–11)

Conveying Eternal Glory

A final "good" that God can bring out of suffering is to give us eternal rewards for our earthly suffering. In fact, bad as the suffering of this world may be, the apostle Paul has told us that the glories of heaven will make our earthly suffering seem "light":

> For our light affliction, which is but for a moment, is working for us a far more exceeding and eternal weight of glory, while we do not look at the things which are seen, but at the things which are not seen. For the things which are seen are temporary, but the things which are not seen are eternal. (2 Corinthians 4:17–18)

CONCLUSION

We began by talking about Hitler, Stalin, and Mao. They had one thing in common. They were atheists. Of course, when you look at the Crusades and the Inquisition, there is no doubt that there is suffering that can be laid at the feet of the institutional church, but (1) it is a candle next to the sun compared to the suffering caused by atheists, and (2) it was not in keeping with the teachings of the New Testament. If the perpetrators of suffering were Christian, which can be strongly doubted, they were not following the teachings of Christ.

Over a hundred years ago, James Russell Lowell was at a gathering where Christianity was being bashed. In response, he said:

> I challenge any skeptic to find a ten square mile spot on this planet where they can live their lives in peace and safety and decency, where womanhood is honored, where infancy and old age are revered, where they can educate their children, where the Gospel of Jesus Christ has not gone first to prepare the way. If they find such a place, then I would encourage them to emigrate there and proclaim their unbelief. (quoted in *What If Jesus Had Never Been Born?*, D. James Kennedy, 238)

Ultimately, however, the final reason for suffering must dissolve into mystery. There is no way for us to grasp it this side of heaven. For most of us, understanding usually comes after the difficulty is over and we look back. So it will be with life. When we look back from the shores of heaven, we will understand and we will accept. God's character and power will be intact. And we will realize that we are not qualified to be God ourselves, and there are times when we must simply bow to Him and let Him be God.

SPEED BUMP!

Slow down to be sure you've gotten the main points from this chapter.

Q1. Where did evil come from?

A1. Evil originated with *Satan* and entered the world with Adam and Eve.

Q2. Why doesn't God remove evil?

A2. God cannot destroy all evil without destroying *humanity*.

Q3. How can God be good and still allow evil and suffering?

A3. An infinite, holy God has thoughts and ways that are *higher* than ours.

Q4. What good can come of evil and suffering?

A4. Evil and suffering are not good, but God can *use* them for good.

FILL IN THE BLANK

Q1. Where did evil come from?

A1. Evil originated with _____ and entered the world with Adam and Eve.

Q2. Why doesn't God remove evil?

A2. God cannot destroy all evil without destroying _____.

Q3. How can God be good and still allow evil and suffering?

A3. An infinite, holy God has thoughts and ways that are _____ than ours.

Q4. What good can come of evil and suffering?

A4. Evil and suffering are not good, but God can _____ them for good.

FOR FURTHER THOUGHT AND DISCUSSION

1. Do you have any speculations as to why Satan would have rebelled against God? Read Isaiah 14 and Ezekiel 28 to see if they give you any ideas.

2. Do you have any speculations as to why Adam and Eve rebelled against God? Read Genesis 3 to see if it gives you any ideas.

3. What do you think is the best answer to the problem of suffering and pain? Or saying it another way, what would you tell a seeker who wanted an honest answer to that question?

WHAT IF I DON'T BELIEVE?

If I don't believe that there is a valid reason for the existence of pain and suffering, I will not be able to accept the goodness of God. If I don't believe that there is mystery involved (that is, the answer may go beyond our information or understanding), then I may be deeply frustrated, believing that a clearer answer is possible, but I am not able to find it.

FOR FURTHER STUDY

1. Scripture

- Isaiah 14:12–15
- Ezekiel 28:15
- Romans 5:12–19
- 2 Corinthians 5:19–21

2. Books

Where Is God When It Hurts? Philip Yancey
For Those Who Hurt, Chuck Swindoll
The Problem of Pain, C. S. Lewis
A Grief Observed, C. S. Lewis
Defending Your Faith, Dan Story
Intellectuals Don't Need God (And Other Modern Myths), Alister E. McGrath
Handbook of Christian Apologetics, Peter Kreeft

7

WHY BELIEVE CHRISTIANITY OVER JUDAISM?

Jesus Christ is the unique and total incarnation of truth, the only way, the only life, and yet we betray his spirit of love when we build a wall between Buddhists, Jews, or Muslims, and ourselves. He is our only Master, and yet without betraying him we can learn from the Greek philosophers, the sages of India, the philosophers of China, or the sacred texts of ancient Egypt.
—**Paul Tournier**

Three major world religions—Judaism, Islam, and Christianity—worship, in concept, the same God: the God of Abraham. A fundamental difference between Judaism and Islam is that in the former the promises and work of God were passed down through Abraham's second son, Isaac, while in the latter the promises and work of God were passed down through Abraham's eldest son, Ishmael. Christianity, of course, is built on Judaism, not on Islam.

To say that all three religions worship the same God is not to say that all three religions are equally valid. As Christians, we believe that God wants the world converted to Christ. But why do we believe this, if all three worship the same God? In this chapter, we will explore what Judaism believes, and why Christianity is to be believed rather than Judaism. In the following chapter, we will look at Islam.

WHAT IS JUDAISM?

Judaism believes that true worship is of Jehovah (Yahweh) only, not Jesus Christ.

It is not easy to define Judaism, because it has changed so much in the last two thousand years. The definition we are using is the broadest possible one, describing historic Judaism and some modern forms of Judaism.

The foundation of Judaism is found in the Old Testament. The father of Judaism is Abraham, with whom God made a covenant around 2085 BC,

91

promising him that he would be the father of a holy nation, set apart from the rest of the world for God's work. This chosen line ran from Abraham to his youngest son, Isaac, and then to Isaac's youngest son, Jacob (whose name was changed to Israel when God made a nation of his sons). Then, it continued through Jacob's twelve sons and their descendants, who formed the twelve tribes of Israel. Divinely ordained circumstances led them from their homeland (near modern Jerusalem) to Egypt, where they lived for four hundred years, most of the time as slaves. During this period in Egypt, they grew from a small family band of less than one hundred to a nation of millions. At the end of the four hundred years, Yahweh led Israel out of slavery in Egypt through the leadership of Moses. Soon afterward, He gave them the Mosaic Law at Mt. Sinai and eventually led them as a nation back into their promised land, approximately the area of modern Israel.

The Law was called the Pentateuch (five books), or the Torah (law), which outlined the history of ancient Israel and contained the laws that were to govern the Jewish people. The story of Israel can be divided into at least five parts: (1) prehistory, including creation, the fall, the period of patriarchs (Abraham, Isaac, Jacob, Joseph), slavery in Egypt, and the exodus out of Egypt into the promised land; (2) conquest of Canaan, the promised land, under the leadership of Moses' successor, Joshua; (3) judges, a four-hundred-year period of loose self-government; (4) united monarchy, under the kings Saul, David, and Solomon; and (5) divided kingdoms of Israel (Northern Kingdom, ten tribes) and Judah (Southern Kingdom, two tribes). The Northern Kingdom was conquered and dispersed by the Assyrians in 722 BC; the Southern Kingdom was destroyed by Babylon in 586 BC. The Babylonian captivity (or Exile) lasted seventy years, after which approximately fifty thousand Jews returned to Jerusalem for a four-hundred-year period that immediately pre-dated the birth of Jesus of Nazareth. For the most part, Judaism accepts the thirty-nine books of the Old Testament as authentic Scripture.

Christianity is built on Judaism.

Throughout God's dealings with Israel in the Old Testament, He made high moral demands on the nation, requiring social and moral justice in return for promises of lavish material blessings if they obeyed or alarming curses if they disobeyed. He required them to sacrifice animals in worship to Him to show that sin required atonement (moral payment). These practices contrasted starkly with those of the nations around them, which were dreadfully immoral and whose gods seemed indifferent to the plight of those who served them. God's goal was to bless Israel for her obedience to Him to such a remarkable degree that other nations would look at Israel and desire to know Yahweh because of what they saw of Him in the national life of Israel. It could be said that God chose Israel not to the exclusion of all the other nations but in order to reach all the others (Psalm 67). Eventually, the Messiah, a descendant of King David, was promised to come to redeem the Jews and the rest of humanity and to reign as king over all the nations.

The Law included three facets: moral, civil, and ceremonial. Moral law governed their personal actions relating to one another and to God. Civil law governed their functioning as a nation. Ceremonial law governed their religious observances before God.

This is the historic picture of Judaism. However, the modern picture is different. In the centuries following the destruction of the kingdoms of Israel and Judah, the temple in Jerusalem was destroyed and therefore the sacrificial system could no longer be observed and the priesthood could no longer function. As a result, the center of Jewish life was transferred

> ## IN THIS CHAPTER WE LEARN THAT . . .
>
> 1. Judaism believes that true worship is of Jehovah (Yahweh) only, not Jesus Christ.
>
> 2. The primary difference Christianity has with Judaism is that Jews do not accept Jesus as the Messiah.
>
> 3. Widely differing opinions on the need for atonement and the nature of the coming Messiah are formidable obstacles for Christians witnessing to Jews.
>
> 4. If Jesus is who He said He was, then one would choose Christianity over Judaism.

from the single temple in Jerusalem to local synagogues (often in homes) that existed wherever there were enough Jews to support one. The synagogues emphasized ritual, prayer, and the study of the Law in place of the previous sacrificial system that surrounded the temple. The Levitical priesthood was replaced by rabbis, who were teachers of the Law; many belonged to the sect of Pharisees who by Jesus' day had developed an elaborate system of rules in addition to the Mosaic Law. The Law and the additional rules were applied in a complex way to every detail of life. Great emphasis was placed on observance of the Sabbath (weekly day of rest), food preparation, dietary rules, and holy days.

Around AD 200, these rules were written down in the Mishnah (sometimes, Mishna), which was placed on a par with the Law. Beyond that, extensive commentaries on both the Law and the Mishnah were developed. The Mishnah and commentaries together were called the Talmud, of which there were two variations, originating in two different locations. These comprise the important writings of Judaism.

Judaism has survived in many countries throughout the world in the last two thousand years by establishing tightly knit communities centered around synagogues. Each community had at least one rabbi. Any Jewish man could be a rabbi if he acquired a good knowledge of the Law and the Talmud, and if he was accepted as a rabbi by the community he wished to serve.

Since the temple and sacrificial system no longer existed, the rabbis began to stress the idea that each Jew had immediate access to God and, as a Jew, needed no conversion or redemption by God. He had already achieved them by being numbered among the people chosen by God.

Judaism rejects the doctrine of original sin, believing that sin is an act, not a condition or a state. Therefore, we have the ability to live according to the Law, and if anyone fails, he needs only to repent. As a result of this emerging view, Judaism has eliminated the need for a personal savior. Many Jews do not anticipate a personal Messiah but a messianic age. Those who do expect a personal Messiah anticipate a political and social leader, not someone to save them from their sins.

Also important to Judaism is the observance of annual festivals and holy days. Rosh Hoshanah is the new year holiday, observed by ten days of solemn penitence (regret for wrongdoing). The tenth and last day of penitence is the Day of Atonement, when Jews acknowledge their sins and pray for forgiveness. The Festival of Booths is a harvest feast marked by great joy. The Passover is the commemoration of the exodus. Hanukkah is the Festival of Lights, which celebrates the dedication of the second temple. And Purim celebrates the deliverance of Jews in Persia from destruction during the reign of Artaxerxes. These holidays commemorate the joys and sorrows of Jewish history.

Judaism rejects the doctrine of original sin.

Modern Judaism is divided into three main branches: Orthodox, Conservative, and Reform. Within the Orthodox branch there is also the ultraorthodox Hasidic (sometimes, Chasidic) movement. Hasidic men wear dark clothing, beards, and long hair with curls at the temples. Orthodox Judaism has not changed much in the last two thousand years. It follows the teachings of the Talmud, strict Sabbath observance, kosher dietary restrictions, and other very detailed rules for everyday life. One reason why this traditional form of Judaism has changed so little is that the Jews have suffered consistent and dreadful persecution and oppression almost wherever they have lived. This has driven them to hold tightly to their cultural and religious traditions in order to preserve their sense of identity within the societies in which they have lived.

A second branch of Judaism is known as Conservative, which lies between Orthodox and Reform. Conservative Judaism observes the feasts and many of the Jewish traditions in an attempt to keep some essentials of traditional Judaism. At the same time, it is open to reinterpreting the Law in favor of more relevant integration with modern thought and culture.

In the last century, especially, many Jewish people have shown a strong tendency to adapt themselves to modern society, especially in the United States. This has given rise to Reform Judaism, a liberal position that has put aside observance of the Talmud and many traditional Jewish practices, as well as the Jewish doctrine of the Messiah and the resurrection of the body. What remains is basically an ethical system built on a God-based philosophy.

> **The link between true Jewish faith and Christianity is strong.**

We see, then, that there is no one definition or understanding of Judaism. It covers a wide range of beliefs and practices.

Christians believe the link between true Jewish faith and Christianity is strong. Christianity subtracts nothing from the Law, but only fulfills it. Jesus said, "Do not think that I came to destroy the Law or the Prophets. I did not come to destroy but to fulfill" (Matthew 5:17). When a Hindu or Muslim becomes a Christian, he is converted. But when a Jew becomes a Christian, he is completed. The first Christians were all Jews, and they did not deny their Jewishness. Rather, they retained and completed it. From this point of view, Christianity is more Jewish than some forms of modern Judaism.

What have we inherited from the Jews? There are five crucial concepts that stand out, which are well outlined in Peter Kreeft's book *Fundamentals of the Faith*.

1. Monotheism. Recorded history reveals little monotheism (only one God) outside of Judaism. The great civilizations of the past, Egypt, Greece, Rome, and a host of lesser ones, were all flagrantly polytheistic (many gods). It seems that the age-old conflict between good and evil gave rise to good and evil gods, and the many challenges of life also seem to give rise to the idea of many gods. This seems reasonable if there is no revelation from God to tell us otherwise. In the midst of a world of polytheism, Jews clearly and staunchly embrace one God, and that God is the God of Christians.

2. Creation. Along with monotheism came the towering story of God's having created the world *ex nihilo*, "out of nothing." The creation myths of polytheistic religions tend to reveal their gods as making the world out of imperfect preexisting stuff, which they say accounts for flaws in the resultant creation, such as evil, pain, and fate. For the Jews, there was only one God. He was all good, and He created the world *ex nihilo*. The consequences of this idea are extremely important. A world created by God is real, not imaginary or a delusion, as it is thought to be in some other religions. It is also a rational world, not a world of nonsense, and, sin aside, it is good. Kreeft said, "Christianity is a realistic, rational, and world-affirming religion rather than a mystical, mythical, or world-denying religion, because of its Jewish source. It is no accident that a disproportionate number of the world's great scientists have been Jewish" (82).

WHY I NEED TO KNOW THIS

I need to know this so that I can understand the wonderful foundation Judaism has provided to Christianity and to give Judaism the respect it deserves, while at the same time being clear on why Judaism is not a sufficient belief system, so that I don't get misled by it.

3. Law. God has created us in His image, and He wants us to reflect the character of God in our lifestyles. God wants us to follow Him out of love, but even if we love Him, we need to understand what it is that He would like us to do. Central, then, to both Judaism and Christianity, is obedience to truth—the keeping of law, if you will. God is not a force or an impersonal influence, but a person. His will is that our will should align with His: "Be holy, for I am holy" (1 Peter 1:16). We love God by keeping His commandments (John 15:10). The law of God should pervade both our personal and corporate lives. This lofty moral law is founded in Judaism, and Christianity builds upon it.

4. Redemption. Each time a sheep, goat, or bull was sacrificed in the temple, it was foretelling our forgiveness by the shed blood of Christ. The Christian can see in each detail of physical Judaism the spiritual reality fulfilled in Jesus. The Law is a tutor, leading us to Christ, said the apostle Paul. No other religion has its god coming to die for the sins of humanity, so that humanity can be forgiven its sins and made perfect, for the sake of full fellowship with that god. It

is an idea so lofty that no human mind would have conceived it. Redemption, so central to Christianity, is a fundamental theme in Judaism.

5. Faith. Both in Judaism and in Christianity, faith does not mean merely intellectual belief, or assent, but faithfulness—that is, fidelity to God, like in marriage. Just as a husband is to be faithful to his wife, so the Jew is to be faithful to his God. This great idea was passed on to Christianity. Sin is the opposite of faith, in the sense that it is the breaking of faithfulness to God. Sin is not just moral or intellectual. It is spiritual, and it breaks one's fellowship with God. Faith is central to Judaism (Abraham was justified by faith in God) and Christianity (without faith it is impossible to please God).

These five critical concepts are rooted in Judaism, and as Christianity flowed out of Judaism they became part of the foundation of Christianity.

WHAT DIFFERENCES DOES CHRISTIANITY HAVE WITH JUDAISM?

The primary difference Christianity has with Judaism is that Jews do not accept Jesus as the Messiah.

There are a number of differences between Christianity and Judaism that keep Christians from accepting Judaism as an acceptable belief system, even though they are both founded on worship of the same God. The greatest one, however, has to do with Jesus Christ. Jesus said He came to fulfill the Law, and He was the final sacrifice. All the blood of bulls and goats shed in the Old Testament were but a picture of the reality to be found in Jesus. Now that the "real" has come, the "picture" is to be left behind. He is the way, the truth, and the life. No one comes to the Father but through Him (John 14:6). Jews as well as Gentiles are to bow to Jesus, and if they don't they are not only rejecting Jesus, but also rejecting Yahweh (Matthew 10:40; John 12:44; 13:20). Most Jews reject Jesus, revealing that they do not really accept Yahweh.

> Christianity and Judaism are both closer and farther apart than any two other religions in the world. On the one hand, Christians are completed Jews; but, on the other hand, while dialogue between any two other religions may always fall back on the idea that they may not really contradict each other because they are talking different languages, and about different things, Jews and Christians both know who Jesus is and simply differ about who he is. He is the rock of stumbling (Is. 8:14), and we dare not reduce him to a pebble. (Kreeft, *Fundamentals of the Faith*, 84)

Though all differences between Christianity and Judaism center in the person and work of Christ, it may be helpful to isolate other specific differences. Judaism essentially denies the sinful nature of humanity rooted in original sin. Therefore, Jews see no need of redemption. They see no need to accept Christ's sacrifice of His life on their behalf so that they can be forgiven and united with God. They believe that repentance is necessary only when they fail to live according to the Law. Some repent only once a year, on the Day of Atonement.

Most expressions of Judaism are focused on culture and tradition. Adherence to the fine points of Jewish practice and tradition is emphasized over personal belief in God as a focal point for living daily life. Judaism is often basically an ethical system and a cultural way of life, with God in the background somewhere.

This is a great difference between Judaism and Christianity, and it causes Christians to believe that Judaism is insufficient to make a person right with God.

Great differences exist between Judaism and Christianity.

Jesus claimed to be the Jewish Messiah, whose life fulfilled the Old Testament prophecies. Failure of the Jews to accept Jesus is seen by Christians as a failure to accept the whole point of God's promises to the Jews. God now wants both Jews and Gentiles to become one in Jesus, and for Jews to reject that plan leaves them on the outside of God's redemptive work (Romans 9:6–8). A Jew is lost until he is completed in Christ, just as a Gentile is lost until he is converted to Christ. The real distinction between people, now that Jesus the Messiah has come, is not Jew/Gentile but Christian/non-Christian. There are Hebrew Christians and Gentile Christians. A Jew does not have to give up his heritage to become a Christian. But he does have to accept Jesus as the Messiah.

WHAT OBSTACLES INTERFERE WITH CHRISTIANS WITNESSING TO JEWS?

Widely differing opinions on the need for atonement and the nature of the coming Messiah are formidable obstacles for Christians in witnessing to Jews.

It can be difficult for Christians to have meaningful discussions with Jews regarding issues of faith. One reason is that rabbinical Judaism, the form that arose after the destruction of the temple and the transferral of the focus of Jewish life from the temple to local synagogues and from the priesthood to rabbis, has very different understandings about doctrines that are central to Christianity.

Atonement

Judaism understands that we do not have sin natures; we simply sin. Sin is an act, not a condition. Therefore we have nothing fundamental that we need to be saved from. We just need to repent of our sins and all is well. When Christians speak of atonement for sin and the need for personal salvation, therefore, we cannot assume that our Jewish friends will easily relate or understand our point. It is easy to be talking "apples and oranges."

Rabbi Abraham Joshua Heschel, a venerable figure in Judaism, once said:

> Christianity starts with one idea about man; Judaism with another. The idea that Judaism starts with is that man is created in the likeness of God. You do not have to go far, according to Judaism, to discover that it is possible to bring forth the divine within you and the divine in other men. . . . It is with that opportunity that I begin as Jew. Christianity begins with the basic assumption that man is essentially depraved and sinful—that left to himself he can do nothing. He has to be saved. . . . I have never thought of salvation. It is not a Jewish problem. (quoted by Yechiel Eckstein in *What Christians Should Know about Jews and Judaism*, 66)

We need to understand, then, that from the Christian perspective, Judaism lacks a perception and emphasis on the biblical teaching of the fallenness of humanity and the need for spiritual salvation from sins. They do have a concept of goodness and badness in humanity, but these are only inclinations or tendencies that can be resisted and overcome, so that the power of the human spirit has the ability to conquer bad tendencies within. Evil is seen as using what God has given us in selfish ways. The evil need not be put to death (in contrast to the New Testament teaching in Romans 6:23 that "the wages of sin is death").

> The rabbis taught that death was the result of Adam's disobedience; they did not teach a doctrine of original sin. Nonetheless, they believed that the wickedness of man was great in the earth, and that every imagination of the thoughts of his heart was only evil continually (Genesis 6:5); they explained this condition by positing the existence of the evil tendency. (Dan Cohn-Sherbok, quoted by Green and McGrath in *How Shall We Reach Them?* 132)

Modern Judaism has largely lost any concept of original sin and the need for personal salvation. This makes it difficult to share Christianity with Jews, who often are convinced that we are giving an answer to a problem that doesn't exist. Personal salvation is foreign, complicated, and unnecessary to their understanding of God.

Messiah

Another commonly misunderstood area is their understanding of the Messiah. As we saw, within Judaism belief in a personal Messiah has largely been transformed into a belief in a messianic age. In the more orthodox circles, where a personal Messiah is still envisioned, he is purely a human figure whose contribution will be in political and social areas. The messianic expectations of Jews are quite different from those of Christians.

Rabbi Shmuel Arkush portrayed the person and work of the Messiah in this way:

> The Messiah will be somebody who will rebuild the third Temple, he is somebody who will ingather the exiled Jewish people, he is somebody who will bring peace to the Jewish people and through them to the whole world. These are the three major jobs of the Messiah; and this is what the Jewish people are awaiting as their Messiah. Christianity has taken our patented invention, the Messiah, our man, and elevated him to great heights of being the Son of God, which from a Jewish point of view is unnecessary, and not only unnecessary but in fact it excludes him from being the Messiah. These three jobs are still waiting to be done. (Green/McGrath, 133)

The Messiah, for Christians, is divine. The Messiah for many Jews is only human. These radically different views of the Messiah also make it difficult for Christians to share their faith with Jews who have no expectation or felt need for a Messiah to save them from their sins.

WHY WOULD ANYONE BELIEVE CHRISTIANITY OVER JUDAISM?

If Jesus is who He said He was, then one would choose Christianity over Judaism.

The primary reason someone might trust Christianity rather than Judaism must lie in the character of Christ. If a person finds credibility in who Jesus was, if the material in chapter 3, "Why Believe That Jesus Is God," is found compelling, then Christianity would be chosen over Judaism. If He fulfilled Old Testament prophecies concerning the Messiah, if His teachings are greater than the teachings of any mere human being, if His miracles of healing the sick, giving sight to the blind, and raising people from the dead are compelling, then Christianity must be chosen over Judaism.

In addition, it seems safe to say that Jesus has impacted the world to a greater degree than anyone ever born. The number of people over the last two thousand years who have been, through Christ, the recipients of the blessings of God is staggering. The impact Jesus has made, not just in a purely religious realm, but also through the impact of Christianity on world governments (such as the Roman Empire through Constantine) on medieval Europe, and on modern England and the United States is difficult to overstate. From education to health care to humanitarianism, more good has been done in the world as a result of the influence of Jesus' life than any other single influence.

> The ultimate question is: What does a Jew think of Jesus?

This evidence takes on even greater significance if Jesus is seen as the fulfillment of God's promise to Abraham to bless the whole world through him. God revealed Himself to Abraham in Genesis 12 and gave him a threefold promise: land, descendants, and universal blessing. That is, Abraham and his descendants would be given a promised land, Abraham would be given countless descendants, and not only would God bless Abraham, but He would bless the whole world through Abraham.

However, the third part of this promise has never been fulfilled through Judaism. Jews might contend that it will happen when the Messiah, or messianic age, comes. Yet Christians can look to Jesus and make a claim that the blessing of Abraham to the whole world has come through Jesus, a descendant of Abraham.

Finally, if Jesus rose from the dead, then it would be logical to choose Christianity over Judaism. If Jesus did, in fact, rise from the dead (see *What You Need to Know about Jesus*, chapter 10), then it is reasonable to believe all that Jesus said, and reasonable to choose Christianity over Judaism.

CONCLUSION

If someone who is neither a Jew nor a Christian looks at Judaism and Christianity as competing worldviews, he sees at once fundamental overlap. Both worship the same God, both accept the Old Testament as the Word of God, and both believe in biblical prophecy. At the same time, each one sees stark differences centering on the need for personal salvation and on the person and work of Christ. Thus, one cannot meld the two religions. One must choose between them, and in deciding which, the focus must be on Jesus. If Jesus is who He says He is, Christianity is true. If He is not, then Christianity is not true, and Judaism remains as a potentially valid worldview.

For those of us who are Christians, we need to recognize that in our approach to sharing our faith with Jews, we will probably not get very far if we limit ourselves to trying to prove the Jews are wrong and we are right. Rather, we should try to show the value of Christianity, so that Jews will be motivated to let go of Judaism because they want to grasp Christianity.

Madeleine L'Engle once said, "If my stories are incomprehensible to Jews or Muslims or Taoists, then I have failed as a Christian writer. We do not draw people to Christ by loudly discrediting what they believe, by telling them how wrong they are and how right we are, but by showing them a light that is so lovely that they want with all their hearts to know the source of it."

And so it will likely be with Jews. We have so much in common with them, and we owe Judaism so much, that the decision boils down to Jesus: What will they do with Jesus? We are not always likely to be able to persuade them through argumentation that Jesus is who He says He is. Truth is important, of course, and we should present truth to them. But if not supported with respect and love, it is likely to fall on unreceptive ears.

SPEED BUMP!

Slow down to be sure you've gotten the main points from this chapter.

Q1. What is Judaism?

A1. Judaism believes that true worship is of *Jehovah* (Yahweh) only, not Jesus Christ.

Q2. What differences does Christianity have with Judaism?

A2. The primary difference Christianity has with Judaism is that Jews do not accept Jesus as the *Messiah*.

Q3. What obstacles interfere with Christians witnessing to Jews?

A3. Widely differing opinions on the need for *atonement* and the nature of the coming *Messiah* are formidable obstacles for Christians in witnessing to Jews.

Q4. Why would anyone believe Christianity over Judaism?

A4. If Jesus is who He said He was, then one would *choose* Christianity over Judaism.

FILL IN THE BLANK

Q1. What is Judaism?

A1. Judaism believes that true worship is of ＿＿＿＿＿＿ (Yahweh) only, not Jesus Christ.

Q2. What differences does Christianity have with Judaism?

A2. The primary difference Christianity has with Judaism is that Jews do not accept Jesus as the ＿＿＿＿＿＿.

Q3. What obstacles interfere with Christians witnessing to Jews?

A3. Widely differing opinions on the need for ＿＿＿＿＿＿ and the nature of the coming ＿＿＿＿＿＿ are formidable obstacles for Christians in witnessing to Jews.

Q4. Why would anyone believe Christianity over Judaism?

A4. If Jesus is who He said He was, then one would ＿＿＿＿＿＿ Christianity over Judaism.

FOR FURTHER THOUGHT AND DISCUSSION

1. What do you think are the most important similarities between Judaism and Christianity?

2. What do you think are the most important differences between Judaism and Christianity?

3. What do you think is the most persuasive argument on why Christianity is to be believed over Judaism?

WHAT IF I DON'T BELIEVE?

If I don't understand what Judaism is, I may not have a proper respect for it. At the same time, if I don't believe that Judaism has fatal flaws, I could get deceived into thinking that, because Jews and Christians worship the same God, Jews do not need Jesus.

FOR FURTHER STUDY

1. Scripture

- Matthew 5:17
- John 13:20
- John 14:6
- Romans 9:6–8

2. Books

Cults, World Religions, and the Occult, Kenneth Boa
Fundamentals of the Faith, Peter Kreeft
How Shall We Reach Them? Michael Green and Alister McGrath
Answers to Tough Questions, Josh McDowell

CHAPTER 8

WHY BELIEVE CHRISTIANITY OVER ISLAM?

Jesus differs from all other teachers; they reach the ear; but he instructs the heart; they deal with the outward letter, but he imparts an inward taste for the truth.
—**Charles Haddon Spurgeon** **(1834–1892)**

slam is one of the fastest growing religions in the world. Its rapid growth, along with the dramatic attention Islam has received as a result of radical Islamic terrorism, has brought this previously little-known and little-understood religion into bright worldwide scrutiny. Because of the difference between militant Islamists and moderate Islamists, many people are confused and uncertain as to what to believe about Islam.

What is Islam? What does it believe? How does it compare with Christianity? These questions are the subject of this chapter.

WHAT IS ISLAM?

Islam, based on the teachings of the prophet Muhammad, claims to worship the same God as Judaism and Christianity (the God of Abraham) but does not believe in essential Christian doctrines.

Allah is the Arabic term for God. The word *Islam* means "surrender," or "submission," to the will of Allah. *Muslim* (or *Moslem*) is related to this word and means "one who submits." "Islam" refers to the religion, and "Muslim" refers to the one who embraces Islam.

Islam combines elements from both Judaism and Christianity. Muslims accept Noah, Abraham, Moses, David, John, Jesus, and others as legitimate prophets of Allah. They also claim that Muhammad is the last and greatest of the prophets, that

105

the Qur'an (or Koran) is the final revelation from God, and that Islam is the true continuation of the faith of Abraham.

Abraham was the father of two sons, Ishmael and Isaac. Muslims believe they have descended from Ishmael and that Jews and Christians corrupted God's earlier revelations. This led to a restoration of the true faith in Allah's revelations to the prophet Muhammad; therefore, in Islam Muhammad supersedes all prophets, including Jesus, and the Qur'an supersedes all revelation, including the Old and New Testaments.

In understanding Islam, one must understand four things:

Islam is one of the fastest growing religions.

(1) the prophet Muhammad

(2) the Qur'an (Koran)

(3) the five articles of faith

(4) the five pillars of Islam

The Prophet Muhammad

Muhammad was born about 570 years after Jesus in the Arabian town of Mecca, which was a wealthy trading center linking land and sea trade routes. Muhammad's father died before he was born, and his mother died when he was only six years old. His grandfather then took care of him, but he soon died. Muhammad was then reared by his uncle, Abu Talib. Not much else is known about his early life.

As an adult, he prospered and became a member of a highly regarded merchant's guild at Mecca. He was known as Al-Amin, "the trustworthy one." His business put him in contact with both Jews and Christians, and as a result he acquired a superficial knowledge of their religions.

A wealthy widow, Khadija, put him in charge of her caravans and later married him, though he was probably fifteen years younger than she. Nevertheless, the marriage seems to have been a good one, lasting for twenty-five years until Khadija's death. They had seven children, three boys and four girls. But only one girl, Fatima, survived into adulthood. She was the mother of Hassan and Hussein, who became two venerable patriarchs of Islam.

Muhammad is Islam's main prophet.

Because of his wife's wealth, Muhammad no longer had to work, and he devoted much of his time to meditation and prayer.

Believing that Allah was the one true God, Muhammad was troubled by the idolatry of his countrymen. At the age of forty, he began to have dramatic visions accompanied by seizures. He was not sure if the visions were divine or demonic, but his wife encouraged him to accept the visions. He believed they came from the angel Gabriel, who instructed him to preach Allah's message to the world.

At first, few people were influenced by his preaching. His first converts were his wife, Khadija, his nine-year-old nephew, and his adopted son, who had been a slave. The first convert outside his family was Abu Bakr, a wealthy merchant. There were a meager fifty converts during the first three years of his ministry.

His public ministry drew strong opposition, and he had to flee Mecca for his life. His flight from Mecca in 622, the Hegira (*Hijrah*, or "flight"), is one of the most important dates in Islam. It marks the beginning of the Islamic calendar. Muslims figure their calendars using the initials A.H. ("in the year of the Hegira"). Muhammad withdrew with all his followers—nearly two hundred by now—to the Arabian city of Medina. Most of the people at Medina became his followers, and he became a statesman, legislator, and judge. He used "divine revelations" to establish new laws and governmental policies. He began to conquer other people militarily and force them to submit to Islamic rule.

At first, Muhammad chose Jerusalem as the city his converts should face when praying, and he adopted some Jewish practices. But when the Jews failed to recognize him as a true prophet, Muhammad commanded that prayers be directed toward Mecca.

Muhammad warred almost continuously with Mecca and eventually conquered it, tearing down the idols and establishing Islam as its official religion. By the time of his death in 632, Muhammad and his armies had conquered most of

IN THIS CHAPTER WE LEARN THAT . . .

1. Islam, based on the teachings of the prophet Muhammad, claims to worship the same God as Judaism and Christianity (the God of Abraham) but does not believe in essential Christian doctrines.

2. The primary difference Christianity has with Islam is that Muslims do not accept Jesus as the Son of God.

3. Widely differing opinions on Jesus and the Bible are formidable obstacles for Christians witnessing to Muslims.

4. The gospel story of God's love in Jesus, proven by His miracles, teaching, sacrificial life and death, and glorious resurrection, outshines the message of Islam which knows little of the love of God and a personal relationship with Him.

Arabia. By the eighth century, Islam controlled parts of India, all of North Africa, and parts of Europe. If it had not been for Charles Martel's victory over the Islamic armies at the Battle of Tours in 732, Islam might have conquered all of Europe. Today, Islam has approximately one billion followers, up from five hundred million just twenty years ago.

The Qur'an (Koran)

The Qur'an is the recognized scripture of Islam. Muslims believe it is the direct word of Allah revealed to Muhammad by the angel Gabriel. The Qur'an is about the same size as the New Testament, and is divided into 114 surahs (or chapters). Apart from the famous opening chapter of the Qur'an, the surahs are arranged according to size, with the larger ones at the beginning. The shorter chapters near the end of the Qur'an are from the earlier part of Muhammad's mission.

The Qur'an is the authoritative Islamic book.

An important Muslim claim about the Qur'an is that it is an eternal book, engraved in Arabic on tablets of stone located in the "seventh heaven." The Arabic language is therefore considered to have a status above all other languages. Despite Muslim devotion to the Qur'an, there are contradictions between parts of the Qur'an, and legitimate questions to ask about the human origins of the Qur'an in Muhammad himself.

The first surah is a prayer to Allah used daily by devout Muslims. It has a place similar to the Lord's Prayer for Christians:

Praise be to Allah,
The Lord of the worlds,
The merciful,
The compassionate,
The Lord of the Day of Judgment.
It is you we serve,
And to you we call for help.
Guide us in the straight path,
The path of those on whom you have bestowed good,
Not on those on whom anger falls,
Or those who go astray.

Some people who are not well acquainted with Islam incorrectly believe that Muhammad is worshiped. Muslims dislike being called Muhammadans because they are not worshipers of Muhammad but of Allah. The Qur'an commands obedience to Muhammad, however, and his life is taken as a model of piety.

Devout Muslims revere the Qur'an and recite verses from it five times a day in their prayers, and they try to learn as much of it by memory as possible. In fact, some Muslim clerics have memorized the entire book! No devout Muslim would ever make a noise while the Qur'an is being read aloud.

The Five Articles of Faith (What Muslims Believe)

1. Allah. Allah is the one true God. Muslims believe that since God is one the Christian doctrine of the trinity is polytheistic. Allah is omnipotent (all-powerful), omniscient (all-knowing), and so beyond us that He is virtually unknowable. Since we cannot know Him, the best we can do is obey Him.

Islam often interprets the sonship of Jesus literally, claiming that Jesus was the result of a physical union between God and Mary. Jesus is presented in the Qur'an as a great miracle worker and one of the greatest prophets, but He is not to be viewed as the Son of God.

Since Allah cannot be known but can only be obeyed, judgment and justice are basic to Islam. Allah demands obedience to all commands, and all human actions are either rewarded or punished.

Most Muslims believe that Allah created heaven and earth in six days. Adam and Eve were created in Paradise, in one of the heavens. They were deceived by Satan, but God forgave them, and they were sent to earth to begin the human race. Children are born free of sin, and if they die as children they go to live in Paradise.

2. Scriptures. Jews and Christians are regarded by Muslims as "people of the book." They believe that the law was revealed to Moses, the psalms to David, the gospel to Jesus, and the Qur'an to Muhammad. They believe that Jews and Christians changed and corrupted their own Scriptures, so Allah sent the Qur'an as the final revelation to humanity. The Qur'an is believed to be eternal as is Allah.

WHY I NEED TO KNOW THIS

I need to know this so that I will not be deceived into thinking that Islam is an acceptable avenue to God, or that, since Islam claims to worship the God of Abraham, Muslims believe the same thing as Christians.

Monotheism is central to Islam.

3. Prophets. Allah has sent many prophets to guide us. Some say there are as many as ten thousand. The Qur'an mentions twenty-eight, most of whom are found in the Old and New Testaments. One cannot deny the prophets and be a Muslim. Jesus, they believe, was the greatest of the prophets until Muhammad came. Jesus was sinless, but not divine. The role of the prophets was to remind people of the day of judgment and to guide them in right and wrong, so that they could go to Paradise and not to hell when they die.

4. Angels. Muslims believe that there are good angels and bad angels (demons), and great importance is placed on them. Anyone who denies them is an infidel. Good angels are created out of light and serve Allah. The greatest angel is Gabriel, who revealed Allah and the Qur'an to Muhammad. He strengthened Jesus during His temptations.

Muslims usually believe they are assigned two angels, one to record his good deeds and one to record his sins. Two angels visit every newly buried corpse in its grave. They make the corpse sit up, and they ask questions of it regarding the faith. If the answers are satisfactory, it is allowed to sleep in peace. If the corpse does not confess Muhammad, they beat it. Animals can hear the cries, but humans cannot. Demons are created out of fire, and good and bad angels battle for believers' souls.

5. Judgment Day. Judgment day is a fundamental theme of Islam. On the last day, an angel will sound a trumpet and people will be resurrected to heaven or hell, with each person's total life deeds determining the place. Some believers will be saved immediately; others must suffer in hell for a while and then go to heaven.

Muslims believe in a day of judgment.

According to the Qur'an, heaven is a place of sensual delights where there are beautiful women, couches covered with beautiful fabrics, and delightful food and drink. This male version of heaven seems dominant in Islam, but Muslim women are assured the wonders of paradise as well.

Some Muslims believe in a sixth article of faith, "The Decrees of Allah," in which Allah has ordained everything that will come to pass. So there is a pervading sense of fate among Muslims. The feeling that fate cannot be escaped has, some believe, held Islamic nations back from cultural, scientific, and technological advancement.

The Five Pillars of Islam (What Muslims Practice)

1. Creed. The creed is a simple one, but it must be recited with conviction several times daily: "There is no god but Allah, and Muhammad is Allah's messenger." Reciting this simple creed is sufficient to enroll one in the ranks of Islam.

2. Prayer. Devout Muslims observe prayer five times a day (upon rising, at noon, in midafternoon, at sunset, and before bed). These prayers are compulsory for men and women over the age of ten, and they may be said publicly or privately. It is generally considered to be better to say them in a mosque, which most men do, but women often do not because of domestic duties. Muslims always pray facing Mecca.

Before they pray, they must ritually cleanse themselves with water, washing face, arms, hands, ankles, and feet with clean water. If there is no water, sand can be used on the face and arms. Just before each prayer, a muezzin (the one who calls the faithful to prayer five times a day) sings and cries from the minaret of the mosque, "Allah is the greatest. I bear witness that Muhammad is the messenger of Allah. Come to prayer. Come to prosperity. Allah is the greatest."

> **Devout Muslims pray five times a day.**

3. Fasting. For the devout Muslim, fasting includes more than "not eating." It means abstaining from eating, drinking, smoking, and sexual relations. For one month each year, during the holy month of Ramadan, all men, women, and children over the age of ten must fast during the daylight hours. They may rise early before dawn to eat breakfast and eat again as soon as it gets dark. It is intended primarily to be a spiritual and moral discipline so that physical desires can be conquered.

4. Almsgiving. At one time, almsgiving was a voluntary practice, but it has since become an obligation under Islamic law. It is the duty of Muslims to give to the poor. This pillar is based on teaching in the Qur'an and the instruction and example of Muhammad.

5. Pilgrimage. Once in a person's lifetime, if able to afford it, he or she is to take a pilgrimage to Mecca during the month of pilgrimage. The trip helps Muslims attain salvation. Saudi Arabia forbids the entry of any non-Muslim into Mecca at any time.

Some Muslims claim a sixth pillar known as *Jihad*. This term refers both to "holy war" involving physical battle and to rigorous spiritual discipline. The use of physical force is sanctioned in the Qur'an (Surah 2:163–64; 9:5, 29). Muslims believe that those who die in a holy war gain instant paradise. However, Muslims can call for *Jihad* against each other, as in the eight-year war between Iran and Iraq.

There are additional practices that are part of Islam, but which do not have the status of the five pillars and *Jihad*. They include circumcision, the veiling of women, and prohibitions against eating pork, drinking alcohol, gambling, eating meat killed by strangling, and lending money on interest. Islam also includes the usual moral prohibitions, such as against lying, cheating, stealing, adultery, and murder.

Since Muhammad did not believe in any separation of church and state, Muslims place great importance on obedience to Islamic law. For example, the death sentence by Iranian leader Ayatollah Khomeini on Salman Rushdie for his infamous book *The Satanic Verses* arose out of Khomeini's ruling about Muslim laws on blasphemy. The emphasis on law in Islam has led to legalism and to turmoil in Muslim countries over who has the proper interpretation of the law.

Just as Christians are not united in all beliefs regarding their faith, so it is within Islam. There are two major sects within the Muslim faith, and they are sharply divided over some aspects of their faith. The Sunnis represent "orthodoxy" simply because they comprise about 90 percent of all Muslims. Sunni Muslims believe that Muhammad's successor was to be someone from his tribe and that Islamic leaders are to be elected by consensus. These leaders (in history, known as caliphs) do not have the authority of Muhammad.

The Shiite sect believe that the only rightful successor to Muhammad must be a descendant of Muhammad. They believe in the doctrine of an infallible, divinely appointed Imam (successor of Muhammad) to whom Allah entrusted the guidance of his people. This continued until the last or twelfth Imam, who disappeared in 874. Shiite Muslims believe that he is in a state of supernatural suspension until he returns as the messiah at the day of judgment.

WHAT DIFFERENCE DOES CHRISTIANITY HAVE WITH ISLAM?

The primary difference Christianity has with Islam is that Muslims do not accept Jesus as the Son of God.

Muslims believe that Jesus was born of the virgin Mary, but they do not believe that Jesus was the Son of God, or claimed to be. While they believe He was sinless, they do not believe that He died on the cross. Rather, Allah let Jesus escape Calvary by letting someone else die in His place! Therefore, of course, they do not believe that He died to atone for our sins, or that salvation is experienced by grace through faith in Jesus.

WHAT OBSTACLES INTERFERE WITH CHRISTIANS WITNESSING TO MUSLIMS?

Widely differing opinions on Jesus and the Bible are formidable
obstacles for Christians witnessing to Muslims.

At first glance, when it is recognized that both Christianity and Islam claim to worship the same God (the God of Abraham), it would be easy to assume that Christianity and Islam are not all that different. Yet, besides the Muslim view of Jesus, the differences between the two faiths are fundamental and profound. If one is a knowledgeable and devout Muslim, he has rejected all that is vital to Christianity.

First, Islam rejects the Bible, both Old and New Testaments, believing that, while at one time they may have been the Word of God, they have been so corrupted through copying and translating that they are no longer reliable. Christianity, of course, believes that the Bible is the Word of God, without error in the original manuscripts, and that the copying of manuscripts over the ages has been so exacting that the variations in texts are

Christianity and Islam disagree on fundamental points.

extremely few and affect no major doctrine. The Bible is the Word of God and reliable revelation from Him.

Second, Christianity also believes that Jesus is the divine Son of God, the second member of the Trinity, along with the Father and the Holy Spirit. Jesus died on the cross to offer salvation to humanity; He was buried, and on the third day He rose from the dead. We cannot be saved by good works (Ephesians 2:8–10; Titus 3:5) but by grace through faith in Jesus. Our good works, which are important, are signs that we have already been saved, not ways to get saved. All this, Islam rejects. The Qur'an rejects the divinity of Jesus, the Trinity, Jesus as the incarnation of God, atonement for sin, and literal resurrection. These are thought to be delusions, conjecture, error, or fraud.

WHY WOULD ANYONE BELIEVE CHRISTIANITY RATHER THAN ISLAM?

The gospel story of God's love in Jesus, proven by His miracles, teaching, sacrificial life and death, and glorious resurrection, outshines the message of Islam, which knows little of the love of God and a personal relationship with Him.

In defense of this claim, I draw your attention to several different elements in the Christian's worldview.

1. Islam denies the divinity of Jesus, as well as His resurrection, which is directly related to His divinity. Jesus said He was God, and as proof He prophesied that He would be killed and rise from the dead three days later. If the resurrection is true, then it is reasonable to believe that everything Jesus said is true, including His divinity.

Islam denies the divinity and resurrection of Jesus.

   Muslim denial of the death and resurrection of Jesus is rooted in dogmatic opinion, not on historical investigation. Even secular historians do not dispute that Jesus died on a cross. Unfortunately, Muslims simply choose to ignore both biblical and secular evidence about His death. This leads, tragically, to their neglect of interest in the greatest news ever announced: Jesus has risen from the dead.

2. The Muslim charges of corruption in the Bible do not fit reality. There are, by far, more copies of manuscripts of the Bible than any other ancient document. These manuscripts have been analyzed and compared more than any other work from the time of Plato. The variations among them are few and minor and affect no central teaching of Christianity.

3. Muslims claim that the Qur'an is eternal, part of a larger document that exists in heaven near the throne of Allah. Written in Arabic, this Islamic scripture is considered pure and infallible. Yet scholars have identified many words in the Qur'an that are of modern origin.

   The Qur'an is sprinkled with words borrowed from Persian, Hebrew, Greek, Latin, Syric, and Coptic that date it to a particular epoch and culture. A renowned classical exegete of the Qur'an, Julad-ud-Din Sayutte, provides a list of 122 loan words from foreign languages (*How Shall We Reach Them?* 150).

4. The Qur'an contains myths and apocryphal (untrue, invented) information, including the following:

- Solomon talked with birds and ants (27:15ff).
- Three men slept in a cave with a dog for at least three hundred years (18:10–25), which is an apocryphal Christian fable.
- Jesus spoke from the cradle (19:29–30). He made birds out of clay and gave them life (3:49). This material is found in the apocryphal *Infancy Gospel of Thomas*.

In addition, there is information in the Qur'an that directly contradicts the Bible. It says that Mary, the mother of Jesus, was the sister of Aaron (19:28). It also says that she was the daughter of Imran, or Amram (3:35–36), which would make her identical to Miriam, the sister of Aaron. It is not difficult to validate that Mary and Miriam are separated by approximately fifteen hundred years. It is also stated that Noah's wife and one of his sons perished in the Flood (in direct contradiction to the Bible).

5. When you compare Christianity with Islam, you are pitting Jesus' words against Muhammad's. By looking at the character of the two people, one is forced to decide which one has the greater credibility. It is not difficult for me to believe in Jesus over Muhammad. The character, words, and works of Muhammad are decidedly human.

The character, words, and works of Jesus are beyond what have ever been witnessed of a mere mortal.

Napoleon once said that Jesus' mode of gathering people to Himself was much different from the way Julius Caesar, Alexander the Great, and he (Napoleon) gathered people, which was by fear. Jesus gathered people through love.

Alexander, Caesar, and I have been men of war, but Christ was the Prince of Peace. The people have been driven to us; they were drawn to him. In our case there has been forced conscription; in his there was free obedience.

This is a very significant point. Jesus taught conversion by faith. While Muhammad may not physically have forced people to convert to Islam, his love of the sword provided a political and social pressure to convert that was sometimes extreme.

Fundamentally, the teaching of Jesus is about the gracious love of God as Father, who loved lost humanity so much that He sent His eternal Son to die for us. One of the most tragic things about the Qur'an is that it lacks any deep understanding of the grace and love of God. In fact, the Qur'an fails to state even once that "God is love."

CONCLUSION

When they are growing up, people tend to believe what those around them believe. Thus, people who grow up in Islamic countries tend to believe in Islam; people who grow up in Hindu countries tend to believe in Hinduism; people who grow up in Christian countries tend to believe in Christianity. Since each religion teaches that it is "reasonable" and each has scholars who defend the particular religion, how do we decide the truth?

It is extremely important that each of us has a heart for sincerity and truth, asking God to lead us into truth. If we come to any religion with a presupposition as to whether or not it is true, we can find whatever information we need to support the presupposition. I came to a point in my life when I was disillusioned with Christianity. I had been a Christian for a few years and became disturbed over the doctrine of hell. I didn't understand why, if He didn't need to, God created hell, if He knew that even one person would end up in hell as a result of the creation. And, since I had become a Christian during a time of personal crisis and grabbed at the closest thing I knew that I thought would hold me up, I decided to rethink my commitment to Christianity. Maybe it wasn't true. Or maybe it wasn't the only truth. So I investigated all major world religions as well as atheism.

Jesus taught conversion by faith not by force.

Islam had the credibility of claiming to worship the same God as two other major world religions, Christianity and Judaism, so in my mind it needed serious investigation. But when I looked at it, it just seemed to be lacking. It seemed to be a religion that a human could have conceived of. There was a God who had a standard of right and wrong. If you violated his standard long enough or badly enough, you would finally cross a line and be punished by this God forever. It was reasonable, because it is how human beings tend to act.

Islam doesn't measure up in the lofty themes that are central to Christianity. It doesn't produce the quality of life. It doesn't create the love. And, it doesn't have Jesus.

There is something about Jesus that makes Christianity different from all other religions, and that is the difference between a man-made religion and a

God-offered religion. Is Islam popular? Of course. Millions believe it. But does it measure up to Christianity? Not in my mind.

SPEED BUMP!

Slow down to be sure you've gotten the main points from this chapter.

Q1. What is Islam?

A1. Islam, based on the teachings of the prophet *Muhammad,* claims to worship the same God as Judaism and Christianity (the God of Abraham) but does not believe in essential Christian doctrines.

Q2. What difference does Christianity have with Islam?

A2. The primary difference Christianity has with Islam is that Muslims do not accept *Jesus* as the Son of God.

Q3. What obstacles interfere with Christians witnessing to Muslims?

A3. Widely differing opinions on *Jesus* and the *Bible* are formidable obstacles for Christians witnessing to Muslims.

Q4. Why would anyone believe Christianity rather than Islam?

A4. The gospel story of God's love in *Jesus*, proven by His miracles, teaching, sacrificial life and death, and glorious resurrection, outshines the message of Islam, which knows little of the love of God and a personal relationship with Him.

FILL IN THE BLANK

Q1. What is Islam?

A1. Islam, based on the teachings of the prophet _____, claims to worship the same God as Judaism and Christianity (the God of Abraham) but does not believe in essential Christian doctrines.

Q2. What difference does Christianity have with Islam?

A2. The primary difference Christianity has with Islam is that Muslims do not accept _____ as the Son of God.

Q3. What obstacles interfere with Christians witnessing to Muslims?

A3. Widely differing opinions on _____ and the _____ are formidable obstacles for Christians witnessing to Muslims.

Q4. Why would anyone believe Christianity rather than Islam?

A4. The gospel story of God's love in _____ , proven by His miracles, teaching, sacrificial life and death, and glorious resurrection, outshines the message of Islam, which knows little of the love of God and a personal relationship with Him.

FOR FURTHER THOUGHT AND DISCUSSION

1. What do you think are the most important similarities between Islam and Christianity?

2. What do you think are the most important differences between Islam and Christianity?

3. What do you think is the most persuasive argument on why Christianity is to be believed over Islam?

WHAT IF I DON'T BELIEVE?

If I don't understand what Islam is, I may not have a proper respect for it, especially since it is founded on concern to worship of the God of Abraham. At the same time, if I don't believe that Islam has fatal flaws, I could get deceived into thinking that Muslims do not need Jesus, because Muslims and Christians claim the same God.

FOR FURTHER STUDY

1. Scripture

- Micah 5:2
- John 14:6
- Ephesians 2:8–10
- Titus 3:5

2. Books

Christ and Islam, James A. Beverley
Islam, George Braswell
Answering Islam, Norman L. Geisler and Abdul Saleeb
Their Blood Cries Out, Paul Marshall
God Has Ninety-Nine Names: Reporting from a Militant Middle East, Judith Miller

WHY BELIEVE CHRISTIANITY OVER EASTERN RELIGIONS?

*Jesus is God spelling himself
out in language that
man can understand.*
—**Samuel Dickey Gordon**
(1859-1936)

I will never forget the first time I saw them. They were Hare Krishna disciples, dressed in soft, salmon-colored robes, heads shaved except for a pony tail. They were clinking little cymbals, beating drums, dancing, and chanting, "Hare Krishna, Hare Krishna, Krishna, Krishna, Rama, Rama . . ." They swayed and twirled in ecstasy. I was a first-year student in seminary, visiting a city park one Saturday afternoon, and I had decided I would talk with one of them about Jesus Christ. He was an American, bright and articulate, but we got nowhere. It was as though we had come from two different planets. We spoke the same language, but we didn't come within a hundred miles of understanding each other.

However, if we are going to witness to those who follow Eastern religions, we must learn to understand where they are coming from—why they believe their faith—and offer an attractive alternative in our loving witness to the claims of the Lord Jesus Christ.

WHAT ARE EASTERN RELIGIONS?

*Eastern religions originated in Asia and commonly believe
in karma, reincarnation, and nirvana.*

It is helpful to understand why Eastern and Western perspectives are different. Modern Western thought has its origins in ancient Greece and has therefore been strongly influenced by the rational emphases in thinkers like Socrates, Plato, and Aristotle. Both Jews and Christians have been influenced by the Western philosophical tradition, and hold that the universe has meaning to it, since it is anchored in the wisdom of an all-knowing God who created it. The rise of science can be explained by reference to the Western philosophical tradition in combination with a Judeo-Christian worldview. The Western mind believed it could find "law" in nature because there was a "law-giver." Even though many scientists today do not believe in God, they still believe that there are laws by which the universe works, and this enables us to make scientific and technological advances that have stunned and changed the world. Almost certainly, without this view of nature and God, we would never have discovered penicillin or gone to the moon.

IN THIS CHAPTER WE LEARN THAT . . .

1. Eastern religions originated in Asia and commonly believe in karma, reincarnation, and nirvana.

2. Christianity and Eastern religions see very little in common.

3. Not only religious views, but also basic views on reality separate Christianity and Eastern religions.

4. If one believes that this world is real, and if one longs for meaning and hope based on reality, he will choose Christianity over an Eastern religion.

Eastern thought developed much differently, not being influenced by the kind of rationality that pervades Greek, Jewish, or Christian thought. The Eastern mind does not believe that there is a personal Creator-God, or that the universe and life have the same sense of ultimate purpose and meaning. There is an emphasis on illusion (or *mayo*) in Eastern religions that makes human life seem of no great significance.

One of the reasons why the Eastern cultures have, until recently, remained scientifically underdeveloped may be due to the view that this world is, in one sense, an illusion. It is unlikely that any great scientific or technological advances could take place within such a worldview. Of course, in recent decades, China, Japan, India, and the Koreas have been making significant scientific and technological advances, but that is largely because they have borrowed the Western perspective on science and technology.

The view of this life as illusion also makes it quite difficult for a strictly Western mind to understand a strictly Eastern mind, and vice versa. The vocabulary and concepts of the two views are so foreign to each other that they often cannot even find a beginning point for meaningful discussion.

1. Common Characteristics of Eastern Religions

For our purposes, we can focus on some basic similarities of major Eastern religions compared to the three great monotheistic (one God) faiths, Islam, Judaism, and Christianity. For the most part, the Eastern religions do not believe in a personal Creator-God. The three monotheistic faiths believe that a personal God created beings (angels and humans) distinct and apart from Himself, with a measure of independence from Him. Eastern religions are quite different at this important point. They are largely monistic (all is one, one is all). That is, all things are one; every "part" in the world is just a small percentage of one universal "whole," and this whole is an impersonal god. Any distinctions between things, including personal individuality, is perceived as fundamentally an illusion. This results in a worldview called *pantheism* (all is god). It is a difficult concept to grasp for those who have been reared to believe in a personal Creator-God who made all things distinct.

> **In Eastern religions, the world is an illusion.**

A second similarity among Eastern religions is the belief, noted earlier, that in some sense the human story is one of illusion. This is expressed in Buddhism in terms of the denial of the human "self," or in forms of Hinduism by the emphasis on losing one's individuality in the ocean of Brahman or God. Of course, belief that this world is ultimately illusion is very hard to put into practice.

> This point is well illustrated by the famous story of the rajah (prince or king) who introduced an untamed elephant to his garden as his guru (teacher) walked up the drive, and he was most gratified to see his worthy instructor in an undignified scramble to climb a tree to escape. After the beast was driven off, the rajah welcomed his guru, rubbing his hands with ill-concealed glee and saying, "I see that the master did not hold to the truth that the elephant was only part of the world of illusion." His teacher replied with withering scorn: "I see that you are still lost in the fog of ignorance. What you thought that you saw was an illusory guru, being chased by an illusory elephant up an illusory tree." (*How Shall We Reach Them?* 108)

Third, Eastern religions believe that things that we do are not so much our own actions, but the result of things that happened to us in previous lives. This idea is known as *karma*. Everything is predetermined, based on the events that happened before this current life. This teaching can be expressed quite clearly in terms of cause and effect. Why is a woman raped in this life? Answer: Because she was probably a rapist in a previous life.

Fourth, Eastern religions place great emphasis on reincarnation. Buddhists and Hindus believe that we lived in many previous states in the past, and we are likely to live on in many future states, before we finally reach perfection. Previous incarnations can be as an animal or in another human form, and future incarnations can go either way as well. If a person does something evil in this life, it creates bad karma, and he or she might come back to earth as a bug or pig or demon or criminal.

This concept is difficult for Western minds to grasp, because if one is a bug in one life, how can a bug do anything that will elevate him to a higher form in the next life? However, Hindu and Buddhist belief in reincarnation is as certain as Christian belief in eternal life. So, these kinds of questions would be dismissed by Krishna devotees or by Buddhists as simply ignorance of the fundamental truths of the spiritual way.

Another similarity of most Eastern religions is that salvation means escaping the endless succession of births, sufferings, deaths, and rebirths. When you finally accrue enough good karma, you no longer have to be reborn. You simply enter a high enough existence and merge with the permanent, impersonal reality of the universe. You cease having to be reincarnated and finally achieve a permanent, eternal end to suffering. This is not heaven, for it is impersonal. It is called *nirvana*.

2. Hinduism

Hinduism is difficult to describe because almost anything that can be said about it must be qualified. There are so many different perspectives within it, so many customs, traditions, and concepts, that what may be true of one form of Hinduism may not be true of another. For example, while most Hindus believe that God is impersonal, the Hare Krishna group believes that God is ultimately personal.

Reincarnation is a main tenet of Eastern religions.

It is difficult to know exactly when or how Hinduism came into being, since the historical evidence is scantly documented. It began around 2000 BC, when a light-skinned people known as Aryans swept down from the north and conquered the dark-skinned people of the Indus valley in India. The Aryans brought with them a polytheistic religion of hymns, prayers, and chants, which in time were mixed with the beliefs of the Indian people and written down in what are now called the Vedas. The Rig-Veda is claimed by some Hindus to be the oldest human religious document in existence (1000 BC). Aryan priests had the military power and so established themselves as the uppermost, or "Brahman," class, caretakers of their traditions and scriptures.

More writings were added to the Vedas around 500 BC, which established rigid class distinctions, called the caste system. The four classes of the caste system in Hinduism are, from highest to lowest, *Brahman*, or priest; *Kshatriya*, or warrior and nobleman; *Vaishya*, or peasant; and *Shudra*, or slave. Even today in some parts of India, women and the lowest class are not permitted to hear the sacred Vedas. The top three classes can avail themselves of the Hindu teachings, but the Shudras cannot use them.

Hindus worship many or no gods.

Traditionally, members of the three higher classes saw their lives in four stages. First was the student, second was the married householder begetting sons, third was the middle-aged man retreating to the forest for meditation and reflection, and fourth was the wandering holy man. The third stage was often ignored and the fourth stage was not considered mandatory. For these classes, an individual's goals in life are to become righteous and virtuous; to have material goods; to enjoy life through love, pleasure, and appreciation of beauty; and to have spiritual victory over life.

The different strains of Hinduism vary from the one extreme of philosophical Hinduism, which is so sophisticated that it is impossible for the novice to understand, to the other extreme, animism (worship of spirits). Some Hindus focus on the worship of one god, while most worship several. Most Hindus are pantheistic, believing that "all is god." Salvation is regarded as a blissful state of peace (nirvana), which is achieved through three different possible routes:

1. *Jnana Marga* (or *Jnana Yoga*), the way of knowledge, or salvation by knowledge. It is experienced by those who study and understand the truth of the sacred writings (Vedas and Upanishads), by practicing meditation, by listening to the sages, and by becoming focused on one's union with the universe.

2. *Bhakti Marga* (or *Bhakti Yoga*), salvation by devotion and love to a god (usually Vishnu or Shiva). The emphasis here is on worship, and a personal relationship with god. For most Hindus there is the wish to achieve ultimate union with god, often expressed by the image of a drop of water falling into a massive ocean.

3. *Karma Marga* (or *Karma Yoga*), the way of duty or good works. The disciple must perform good deeds, observe rituals and ceremonies, make sacrifices and pilgrimages, and fulfill other prescribed duties that will allow him to be re-born through thousands of reincarnations until he finally reaches *nirvana*, the state of eternal bliss. This may also involve *Raja Yoga*, a technique of medita-tion that includes great control over the body, such as over breathing, heart-beat, and thoughts.

Salvation, it is said, is experienced by attaining the state of nirvana, which is achieved through transmigration of the soul (continual reincarnation upward until nirvana is achieved). Even a womb on planet earth right now can someday, through death and rebirth, attain life form as a human. Then, it must progress through the higher classes by following its duty to certain things according to the class it is in. These include moral, social, and religious duties, which are vital to the Hindu's upward progress.

3. Buddhism

Buddhism is an outgrowth of Hinduism. The man who founded Buddhism was Siddhartha Gautama, who was born a Hindu, several centuries before Christ. He was born to fortune and high position but did not find his religion or his privileged lifestyle satisfying. He abandoned his family and possessions and wandered the countryside as a beggar monk. He studied the Hindu writings but found little satisfaction in them.

Buddhism began before the time of Christ.

Buddhist legend states that Buddha tried to find sal-vation through the Hindu path of the ascetic. In fact, he is said to have gotten so thin that one could put both hands around his stomach and touch the fingertips over his spine! Legend also states that he finally sat under a tree for forty days and nights, swearing that he would not move until he found enlightenment. At the end of this time, he experienced nirvana, the state of bliss that is the final goal of Eastern religions. From that point, he was known as *Buddha*, "the enlightened one," and began to preach and teach his newfound way of salvation. Buddhism eventually grew to become one of the world's major religions.

Buddhism is similar to Hinduism in some ways and different in others. Buddha rejected the belief that the Hindu writings were divine, for they had been of little help to him in finding salvation. He also denied that humans have a soul or self, and he rejected the Hindu teaching regarding the caste system. Buddha also denied the

the ethical system of Confucianism is the respect that the lesser in any relationship must pay to the greater, whether that is the younger to the older, the son to the father, the wife to the husband, and so on. Through his teachings, Confucius changed a superstitious people who believed in good and bad luck into a moral people who became concerned with right and wrong behavior. *Jen*, the goal of Confucianism, means to be genuinely human, a form of earthly salvation achieved through virtue.

China, Korea, and Japan have been strongly influenced by Confucianism, though its forms vary from country to country. The Chinese emphasize family relationships. The Japanese focus on hierarchical relationships. The role of the feudal lord has been replaced to some extent by the company president. Perhaps this explains the extraordinary success the Japanese have had in the corporate world. The Koreans emphasize relationships among friends in a peer group. The largest church in the world is in Korea, numbering in the hundreds of thousands. Perhaps the cultural background in Confucianism explains why.

There is no emphasis on reincarnation or nirvana in Confucianism. It is more of an earthly ethical system of living than a religion. However, many Confucianists have developed an elaborate system of ancestor worship, which gives it the flavor of a religion. This emphasis on ancestor worship creates a difficult situation for Asian Christians who are torn between respect for their ancestors and unbiblical worship of them.

What adds to the complexity of these three Eastern religions, even Confucianism with its ethical ethos, is the added element of folk customs brought to each. For example, in Chinese Buddhism and Confucianism there is an emphasis on astrology. Chinese people can also be very superstitious about numbers or about the particular direction a building faces. These views get mixed in with classical Buddhism and Confucianism.

WHAT DIFFERENCES DOES CHRISTIANITY HAVE WITH EASTERN RELIGIONS?

Christianity and Eastern religions see very little in common.

The differences between Christianity and Eastern religions are profound. In contrast with the monotheism of Christianity, Judaism, and Islam, the Eastern religions offer a different understanding of the ultimate. Buddhists focus on Buddha as the guide to truth, and deny belief in God. Hindus believe in many gods and goddesses. The Hindu legends that form the core of their scripture are not anchored in historical truth. Even many of the stories about Buddha only surfaced centuries after his death.

WHAT OBSTACLES INTERFERE WITH CHRISTIANS WITNESSING TO FOLLOWERS OF EASTERN RELIGIONS?

Not only religious views, but also basic views on reality
separate Christianity and Eastern religions.

The greatest obstacle that interferes with a Christian witnessing to a follower of an Eastern religion is the enormous difference in how each person views reality. Christians believe in truth, and in a personal Creator-God, and that the world is real. Most Eastern religions do not believe these things. As a result, there is almost no common ground to share ideas and discuss faith. For example, some orthodox Hindus resented the ministry of Mother Teresa and her sister nuns, believing that dying people should be left to die, and that Mother Teresa was interfering with their karma by helping them. Christians and Hindus stare at each other across this great divide and wonder what in the world the other could be thinking. With this lack of common perception and of understanding reality in similar ways, Christians and Eastern religionists find it difficult to communicate even on basic issues.

WHY WOULD ANYONE BELIEVE CHRISTIANITY OVER EASTERN RELIGIONS?

If one believes that this world is real, and if one longs for meaning and hope
based on reality, he will choose Christianity over an Eastern religion.

It is difficult to explain why one person believes in one religion and another person rejects it in favor of another religion. However, religions tend to follow geographic lines. Most of the Hindus, Buddhists, and Confucianists in the world live in Asia. Most Muslims live in the Middle East and North Africa. Most animists live in third world countries. So it seems safe to say that, on the surface, most of the people who embrace a given religion do so because those around them do. Hinduism, therefore, seems perfectly reasonable to someone steeped in it from birth, while it may remain incomprehensible to most Americans.

However, there are Americans who have converted to Hinduism and Hindus who have converted to Christianity. But why would anyone accept Christianity over Eastern religions?

When I had my little crisis over Christianity and went looking for another religion because I was having difficulty embracing the doctrine of hell, I considered Hinduism. But I eventually found it unacceptable on several grounds.

First, Hinduism offered me nothing that I wanted. As far as this world was concerned, I did not need hope for an end to relentless suffering. By comparison to most Hindus, I was living an affluent lifestyle, and I was in good health. I had reason to hope for a good future on earth.

As far as life after death was concerned, the promise of nirvana held no interest for me. I could not even find out what nirvana was, short of a foggy state of bliss in which the relentless cycles of suffering were ended. But would I be conscious? If not, it held little promise for me. I wanted conscious bliss. I wanted a personal God.

WHY I NEED TO KNOW THIS

I need to know this so that I can share my faith intelligently with those who have a background in Eastern religions, and so that I will not be deceived into accepting what they teach.

Second, Eastern religions do not seem to be true to "what is." For example, when I read the Bible, it seemed true to what is. The world it presented was real, not an illusion. Its principles were transferrable to today. Its stories are rooted in careful historical reporting, not in unbelievable legends spread through thousands of years. Further, the Bible holds to a high view of human identity, whereas in both Hinduism and Buddhism there is a fundamental opposition to one's individuality. The Eastern emphasis on karma also fails to give honor to human responsibility in this life. When this doctrine of karma is tied in with the emphasis on illusion, there is something very unreal at work, at least to me.

Then there is Jesus. If you apply every test of historical accuracy to the life of Jesus, tests you would apply to any other historical figure, you must come away saying that Jesus existed, that He died on the cross, and that He rose again from the dead. So what do you do with that? If you believe that the events of this world are real and not an illusion, then you must account for the person of Jesus and His resurrection from the dead. As Josh McDowell has stated so well, it is evidence that demands a verdict. And the verdict is, if you look at the evidence without an anti-supernatural presupposition, then you end up believing, in my opinion, that Jesus lived, was

The evidence for Jesus demands a verdict.

crucified, and rose again from the dead. If He could rise from the dead, then there is powerful reason to believe whatever He taught. He taught that if we believed in Him and accepted Him as our personal Savior, we could be forgiven of our sins and be given eternal life. There is reason to believe it. To me, then, Jesus becomes an insurmountable obstacle to pursuing any religion or belief other than Christianity.

CONCLUSION

I am aware that if an Eastern religion theologian were to enter this debate, things would not be as simple as I have just presented them. Issues would arise that I have not mentioned, and further ideas would be discussed surrounding issues I have mentioned. Penetrating questions would come up that are difficult to answer. But this does not change a single conclusion of mine, or alter in the least my belief in what I have written. If there is a God, if He has communicated to us, and if we can know Him, then there is reason to believe Christianity over Eastern religions. If there isn't, we have no reason for hope, and Eastern religions offer another way of dealing with existence.

SPEED BUMP!

Slow down to be sure you've gotten the main points from this chapter.

Q1. What are Eastern religions?

A1. Eastern religions originated in *Asia* and commonly believe in karma, reincarnation, and nirvana.

Q2. What differences does Christianity have with Eastern religions?

A2. Christianity and Eastern religions see very little in *common*.

Q3. What obstacles interfere with Christians witnessing to followers of Eastern religions?

A3. Not only religious views, but also basic views on *reality* separate Christianity and Eastern religions.

Q4. Why would anyone believe Christianity over Eastern religions?

A4. If one believes that this world is *real*, and if one longs for meaning and hope based on reality, he will choose Christianity over an Eastern religion.

FILL IN THE BLANK

Q1. What are Eastern religions?

A1. Eastern religions originated in _____ and commonly believe in karma, reincarnation, and nirvana.

Q2. What differences does Christianity have with Eastern religions?

A2. Christianity and Eastern religions see very little in _____.

Q3. What obstacles interfere with Christians witnessing to followers of Eastern religions?

A3. Not only religious views, but also basic views on _____ separate Christianity and Eastern religions.

Q4. Why would anyone believe Christianity over Eastern religions?

A4. If one believes that this world is _____ , and if one longs for meaning and hope based on reality, he will choose Christianity over an Eastern religion.

WHAT IF I DON'T BELIEVE?

If I don't believe, I may get deceived into thinking that Eastern religions are acceptable and that Christianity is unnecessarily exclusive. Through ignorance, I may begin to think that, since there are so many people who follow Eastern religions, they are an acceptable worldview. According to the Bible, they are not.

FOR FURTHER THOUGHT AND DISCUSSION

1. If you were going to summarize what Eastern religions tend to believe, what would you say?

2. Can you grasp the appeal that Eastern religions have for people? Why or why not?

3. Do Eastern religions appeal to you? Why or why not?

FOR FURTHER STUDY

1. Scripture

- Genesis 1:1
- John 1:1–12
- John 14:6

2. Books

Death of a Guru, Rabi Maharaj

Fundamentals of the Faith, Peter Kreeft

How Shall We Reach Them? Michael Green and Alister McGrath

Answers to Tough Questions, Josh McDowell

The Gospel and the New Spirituality: Communicating the Truth in a World of Spiritual Seekers, Charles Strohmer

10

WHY BELIEVE CHRISTIANITY OVER THE NEW AGE MOVEMENT?

The more men suppress the truth of God which they know, the more futile, even senseless, they become in their thinking.
—John R. W. Stott (1921–2011)

The United States is now being described as a post-Christian nation; others say that we are living in a post-Christian world. This probably is true about the intellectual and political elite of American and world culture. It is certainly true of the media.

But what is the dominant worldview? It is hard to say. There is no doubt that a rising star in the increasing religious diversity in America, however, is something called the New Age Movement (NAM).

The New Age Movement is difficult to describe and define in a short chapter. Nevertheless, there are a number of characteristics that allow us to get a general picture of this worldview.

WHAT IS THE NEW AGE MOVEMENT?

The New Age Movement is a contemporary spiritual movement that focuses on the restoration of a mystical awareness of humanity's godlike potential and ultimate absorption into eternal oneness with the divine.

The New Age Movement has many similarities with Hinduism. It appears to be a Westernized reshuffling of the Hindu cards, and it is finding a home in Western thought because of disillusionment with Western religions (particularly

IN THIS CHAPTER WE LEARN THAT . . .

1. The New Age Movement is a contemporary spiritual movement that focuses on the restoration of a mystical awareness of humanity's godlike potential and ultimate absorption into eternal oneness with the divine.

2. Christianity and the New Age Movement have very little fundamental agreement.

3. Not only religious views, but also basic views on reality separate Christianity and the New Age Movement.

4. If one wants his faith to be grounded in facts, he will choose Christianity over the New Age Movement.

Christianity and Judaism) and modern materialism. For many years, the worldview of the West (Europe, England, the United States) was founded on biblical truth. We believed in the Bible and that there was a self-existent, supreme Creator-God who was separate from nature and humanity, and who created the world to function with laws that reflect Himself.

However, during the Enlightenment, approximately three hundred years ago, many brilliant and influential thinkers drifted from a biblical worldview to one that seemed more "reasonable" to them. These Enlightenment leaders did not follow the one who said, "I am the light of the world." Rather, they looked to philosophy and human reason as the way of "light" out of the darkness of superstitious beliefs like Christianity.

The Enlightenment project was a dogmatic answer to a period of skepticism that followed the breakup of the Christian worldview after the Reformation. Since Luther doubted the pope, and Calvinists doubted Lutherans, and Anabaptists doubted all three, with Anglicans then in doubt about all four, where was truth to be found? Descartes sought to work his way out of this by starting at square one ("I think, therefore I am") and working toward Christianity. Enlightenment philosophers shared Descartes's trust in human reason but not his ultimate trust in God.

The failure of Enlightenment rationality has led to the relativism and skepticism of postmodernism. It has also led people to be more open to contemporary forms of spirituality like the New Age Movement.

With the anchor chain to truth severed, the ship of human existence was left to drift in whatever direction religious or philosophical speculation took it. That has put many in love with the vision of Hinduism, dressed up in a form that fits American individualism and consumerism.

New Age leaders draw on a long tradition of mystical and occult sources for inspiration.

Beliefs

From this foundation, there are a number of recognizable beliefs in the New Age Movement. First is a belief in the interconnectedness of everything. According to the New Age, the problems of humanity arise out of a failure to recognize the interconnectedness of all life. Because we do not see that we are one with other peoples of the world, we feel free to oppress them or to go to war with them. Because we do not see ourselves as interconnected with nature, we feel free to abuse it, to exploit it. Because we do not see ourselves as a unit of body and spirit, we feel free to neglect or abuse our lives. Because we do not see ourselves as all the same, we divide ourselves over religious beliefs.

> The New Age believes in the sacredness and interconnectedness of all things.

Second is a belief that everything is sacred, in the sense that everything is divine. "All is one and all is God" is an often repeated phrase in New Age literature. New Agers are usually pantheistic in their worldview. This was shown most clearly in Shirley MacLaine's televised version of her life story, *Out on a Limb*. She is told by her spirit guide to face the Pacific Ocean, spread out her arms, and declare: "I am God!"

Third is a belief in the inner resources of human beings to attain wholeness and enlightenment. Since truth comes from the divine spark within, the New Age uses intuition, imagination, creativity, and "right-brain" ways of perceiving truth. To follow one's heart and connect with one's inner guidance is the way to "truth." While external evidence is not always rejected, internal conviction and personal experience are more important than rational argument or logical thought. If a spiritual experience means something to you, then that is what counts. Don't worry about what anyone else says. It

> The New Age believes in the divinity of all things, including people.

is not that the New Age wants to overthrow traditional means of discovering truth; rather, it wants to put the traditional means in its right place, which is subordinate to intuition and inner guidance.

The New Age believes that all religions at their core are the same. Therefore the key is to find that core and not quibble about the particulars. Aldous Huxley, an articulate spokesman for an early version of New Age thought, has written:

> The everyday world and our personal consciousness are manifestations of an underlying divine reality. . . . Human beings can realize the existence of the Divine Ground "by a direct intuition, superior to discursive reasoning." . . . We possess a hidden higher self, the spark of divinity within the soul, which reflects this transcendental reality in our lives. . . . This awakening . . . is the goal or purpose of human life. (quoted in *How Shall We Reach Them?* 90)

Based on such thinking, New Age belief takes the teachings of a given religion and finds ways of explaining or joining that teaching as New Age thought. This promotes New Age thinking to a stature that it could not otherwise have, for it is then seen as the embodiment of truth that is universal and long-held, rather than as just a current fad.

Variations in New Age Thought and Practice

Not everyone in the New Age Movement believes the same thing; it has variations in belief and style. Christians have tended to portray the New Age as one unified, organized force; rather, it is a collage of diverse interest groups and individuals, with sometimes very competing and different views.

For example, there are groups within the New Age Movement that are preoccupied with supernatural occult power. By occult, New Agers do not mean the worship of Satan. Rather, they look to various eternal spiritual forces for special powers for everything from predicting your financial future to getting a message from your dead grandmother. Famous channelers have made enormous sums of money in allegedly contacting spirits that can offer guidance to followers of the New Age.

WHY I NEED TO KNOW THIS

I need to know about the New Age Movement since it represents one of the dominant religious moods in contemporary times. By understanding the emphases of the New Age Movement I will be able to separate its good and bad teachings, and be a more effective witness as I share my personal story of trust in Jesus Christ.

Channelers often believe that the problem with humanity is that we have forgotten who we are and why we are here. A common phrase is that "we are spiritual beings having a human experience," having chosen at some previous time in our existence to enter the realm of earth to grow through an experience of love and unity while in a state of separation from our divine source.

We have been transformed into acting as though we are beings of earthly matter, and we have come under bondage to the "self," to our desires, to fear and anxiety and ignorance, all because we forgot that this material world is ultimately an illusion. Don't overemphasize the word *illusion*, however. New Agers know the danger of stepping in front of a moving truck.

> **The New Age wants to transform how people view life.**

Other New Agers believe that the most important task is changing society on the level of spiritual consciousness. It is not a matter of secret occult power but an issue of social change. When enough of us see our need for this focus on spirituality, it will tip the scale for all of humanity and the New Age will dawn. However, there are so many unbelievers, so many unwilling or unable to make the transition, that before the New Age can dawn, there has to be massive re-education in almost every sphere of human learning.

To become New Age, in this sense, is to call for a transformation of how we view life. We must support strategies to ensure the health and well-being of our race and our planet. We must no longer remain apathetic about the problems that threaten our world, and we must replace destructive or ineffective values with values that will bring about world peace and well-being.

A third tendency in the New Age is among those who focus on individual or personal well-being and self-advancement, to become "all that we can be." The divine spark is in each of us. We must fan it into a flame, so that we can experience all that our divine potential allows us to, and so get as much out of life as possible.

To do this, we must eliminate the separation between the secular and the sacred and see everything as sacred. New Agers believe that dualism (seeing things as either secular or sacred) causes people to see spirit and matter as having irreconcilable differences. As a result, there is a diminished evaluation of the body, sexuality, emotions, and nature. New Agers attack Christian faith for allegedly believing that since God (sacred) is separate from nature (secular), then nature is to be exploited.

These different emphases in the New Age Movement can lead to internal debate. For example, many of the more refined New Age thinkers were deeply disturbed by the occult or magical elements in Shirley MacLaine's life story. Likewise, New Agers with a sharp social consciousness have little support for the rampant individualism of the New Ager looking for a quick fix from some channeler.

One way to see the overall thrust of New Age thought is to note its emphasis on the unity of body, mind, and spirit. Many New Age seminars and workshops focus on chanting, drumming, dancing, music, meditation, and guided visualization, all of which encourages people to explore the whole "self," which comprises body, mind, and spirit.

Body. The New Age sees the body and mind as directly connected, each influencing and being influenced by the other. Modern medicine, which tends to treat the body by itself without regard for the mind, is seen as inadequate at best and destructive at worst. The body is not merely a biochemical machine, a purely material entity.

Therefore, to the New Age, consciousness is not confined to the brain, but is present in every self through "neuropeptides." A New Age cliché says, "Where awareness goes, energy flows." As a person brings his awareness and mental focus to a part of the body that is in discomfort or needs healing, he can direct the flow of bodily energy to the needed place that will stimulate healing. It also allows for the possibility of paranormal or psychic healing from other people.

Mind. The New Age believes that there are influences in our past and present that are not perceived by us, and they limit our potential as human beings. Therefore, the New Age champions personal growth and development. It is believed that if these influences that hinder us can be brought to the conscious surface, and recognized and identified, we can be freed from their influence and become all that we have the potential to be. Avenues such as group therapy, inner-child exploration, past-life regression therapy, psychotherapy, and other methods strive to bring to the conscious level the various influences that are directing our thoughts and behavior, so we can overcome them. They commonly employ methods to tap into the subconscious, such as hypnosis, guided imagery, interpretation of dreams, and dream therapy. The goal is to no longer be held captive to unconscious influences that have been put in place by culture, family, and personal experience. We can and must create our own reality.

The New Age sees a unity of body, mind, and spirit.

Spirit. The New Age emphasizes that we must connect with our true self, our higher self, our divine self, our inner self. This inner self is also referred to as "source," God, the spirit, the heart, or the self. This true inner self is characterized by peace, love, joy, and immortality. This inner self, which contains the spark of the divine, is the essential nature of all things. All reality is interconnected by a divine life force, or a divine intelligence, often referred to as God. But it is not the God of the Bible; it is an impersonal force.

As the individual gets in touch with this divine inner self, acting out of the truth and strength found there, he will achieve peace, love, joy, and harmony with himself and with all of creation. Therefore, the New Age person ought to try always to discern what God (the all-pervasive life force) is trying to teach him in every situation, because there is always a purpose. The sooner you discern it, the sooner you can align yourself with the great purpose, and achieve the harmony with self and creation that is the goal of life.

Much of the teaching of the New Age Movement is focused on guiding people into a conscious awareness of their inner divinity so that they can transcend their problems and find purpose and meaning in life.

WHAT DIFFERENCES DOES CHRISTIANITY HAVE WITH THE NEW AGE MOVEMENT?

Christianity and the New Age Movement have very little fundamental agreement.

The tendency among evangelical and fundamental Christians is to discount everything about the New Age Movement as having come from the pit of hell. However, even though the New Age Movement may be fundamentally flawed, there are some elements of truth and wisdom in it with which Christians need not disagree.

For example, the New Age emphasis on the unity of all things has a seed of truth to it. Everything God has created is to be treated with respect. We should respect all people because they are created in the image of God. We are not one with each other in the same sense that the New Age Movement asserts, but there is the brotherhood of man. We are all created by the same Creator. We are all descended from the same parents. And we are all to love one another as God has loved us.

We are also to respect the earth on which we all live. New Age people respect the earth because they believe we are one with it. Christians do not believe that. We are distinct and separate from the earth. The earth was created for our use, but that does not mean we are free to exploit it. If we treat it disrespectfully, it will boomerang on us, as all sin does, and come back to haunt us. All God's creation is interconnected, and we cannot sin in one part of it without its affecting the whole. Whatever we do to nature and the environment we will eventually do to ourselves. If we continually foul our own nest, we will pay the price. God does not allow us to play fast and loose with any part of His creation. It must all be treated with respect and nurtured as a resource, not because we are one with it but because God has given it to us for our use, and we are to be good stewards of it.

We are even to treat animals with respect, not because they are sacred and on an equal plane with humans, as the New Age Movement says, but because "a righteous man has regard for the life of his animal" (Proverbs 12:10 NASB). This does not mean we treat animals exactly the same as we treat humans. We can eat animals (Leviticus 11). But it does mean that we are to have regard for the life of animals and not do unnecessary harm to them.

Regarding personal health, the New Age Movement is often more enlightened than some Christians. More and more scientific evidence is documenting the interrelatedness of the body and the mind. We are a whole being. What we do with one part of us affects every part of us. We should treat our bodies with respect by eating properly and taking care of our bodies as a matter of stewardship. The body was given to us by the Lord, and He intends for us to treat it with respect.

Regarding the pursuit of their inner lives, many in the New Age Movement are more enlightened and disciplined than Christians. Christians are to spend time feeding their mind on truth, praying to the Lord, and meditating on His attributes and His Word. But many are careless and undisciplined in these habits.

Finally, the New Age Movement is trying to get the Western world to bring the spiritual dimension of life back into focus. For too long, they contend, we have treated humanity as though it were a biochemical machine, body only, no soul. We have a soul, they claim, and we must begin to live, think, and act as though we do. Our failure to do so has caused much of the trouble we are currently in. Many Christians would agree with this.

Having recognized some positive aspects of the New Age Movement, Christians must still reject what is not positive. There are many serious and pronounced differences that Christians have with the New Age Movement.

New Age people want to recover the spiritual.

God. Christians believe in a personal, supreme Creator-God. The NAM does not. For the NAM, God is an impersonal, universal force or consciousness. Jesus is not recognized as the only Son of the only God. He is not the only Savior and Lord. The New Age appropriation of Jesus amounts to betrayal with a kiss. New Agers do not usually care to discover the historical, biblical picture of Jesus.

Reality. Christians believe that what we see around us is real and that truth exists and can be known. The NAM believes that all is one, that what is around us is an illusion, that reality is our own personal creation, and that truth lies within and is subjective. Once you have done away with a personal God who reveals truth and morality to humanity, there can be no objective truth.

Salvation. Salvation is not seen as salvation from sin and from the consequences of sin, such as eternal separation from a personal Creator-God. Rather, salvation in the biblical sense is seen as unnecessary because there is no sin. Sin is considered a concept that creates negative self-esteem. This is why one New Age leader dismissed evil one time by saying that it was "just 'live' spelled backwards." Salvation in the New Age sense is usually viewed as a matter of creating and amassing good karma throughout many reincarnations until one evolves into a state of eternal bliss that ends the cycles of reincarnation.

> **Christians and New Agers differ greatly in their views of reality.**

There are other differences, but suffice it to say that there is little agreement between Christians and the New Age Movement on fundamental issues such as God, life, death, and the afterlife.

WHAT OBSTACLES INTERFERE WITH CHRISTIANS WITNESSING TO FOLLOWERS OF THE NEW AGE MOVEMENT?

Not only religious views, but also basic views on reality separate Christianity and the New Age Movement.

The greatest obstacle that interferes with Christians witnessing to followers of the New Age Movement is the enormous difference in how both parties view reality. Christians believe in objective truth, and in a personal Creator-God, and in His final revelation in Scripture, and in Jesus Christ. New Agers do not. As a result, there is almost no common ground to share ideas and discuss faith.

In addition, since the New Age Movement does not believe in an objective orientation to truth, there is often almost no benefit from laying out logical arguments, or appealing to evidence, or showing points of agreement and disagreement.

Nevertheless, the Christian can share his faith with a follower of New Age values by telling of his experience with the Lord and the Scriptures and with other Christians, as well as answers to prayer. The New Ager will respect your experience and perception of reality and may be motivated to give Jesus a chance.

WHY WOULD ANYONE BELIEVE CHRISTIANITY OVER THE NEW AGE MOVEMENT?

If one wants his faith to be grounded in facts, he will choose
Christianity over the New Age Movement.

It is difficult to talk about why one would choose Christianity over the New Age Movement because the reasons one gives only carry weight with someone who has the same values as the one giving the reasons. Reasons based on information and logic are only acceptable if someone values information and logic. But if someone has already decided that information and logic are not sufficient grounds for "knowing" anything, then little can be said.

Nevertheless, I believe there are reasons to believe Christianity rather than the New Age Movement, and I will give my personal reasons.

First, the New Age Movement is not based on verifiable information. It is rooted in Hinduism, which is grounded in unhistorical religious speculation. There is no evidence for reincarnation or karma. There is anecdotal evidence for reincarnation, of course, such as when someone has a dream and remembers that in a past life he was a Scottish warlord. But I want more than that if my eternal destiny rests on the decision.

In the New Age view, there is no personal God or objective truth.

The New Age option offers a terrible risk in its dismissal of a personal God who will judge us. There is a price to be paid in rejection of concern for objectivity and evidence. What if the New Ager is wrong? The wager I make with my life is too great for me to choose the New Age path. If someone else is comfortable with that, I can't change his mind, but don't ask me to make the same decision based on so little evidence.

When I look at the universe, when I look at nature, when I look at humanity as distinct from non-humanity, when I ponder the nature of eternity and matter and time and space, something deep down within me says that there might be a God. There probably is a God. I can't prove it, but I'm not going to bet my soul, if I have one, on intuition, emotion, and ancient or modern speculation. If there is sufficient evidence to suggest that there might be a personal, supreme Creator-God to whom I am accountable, then I'm going to forget about karma and reincarnation. I'm going to serve the Creator-God.

By destroying the link with objective truth and reality, New Agers (and Hindus and many others) destroy the very basis for knowledge and stability. If we cannot know anything for sure, we are thrown, like wheat chaff in a strong wind, into a whirlwind of relativity. Life becomes nonsensical, meaningless, and futile. There is an enormous cost to New Age moral subjectivism. We harm the very concepts of right and wrong, good and bad.

New Agers say they believe in the inherent "goodness" of humanity, but the very definition of goodness implies morality. So, whose morality? If what New Agers call "evil" is called "good" by someone else, how can the New Agers quarrel with it? Obviously, if they wish to be consistent to their view, they cannot.

The New Age philosophy is not a philosophy that can sustain meaningful individual existence if taken to its logical conclusion. Nor can it sustain meaningful social life. The only way the New Age philosophy can exist is if, like a parasite, it lives off the host of a Judeo-Christian ethic that lends its morality and social stability that keeps strong people from victimizing the weak.

Third, since the New Age Movement is fairly new, it has not had time to demonstrate its impact on society, but its father, Hinduism, has had plenty of time, and the record is not good.

The history of India, for example, is a dismal testimony to the value of Hinduism. Riddled with disease, starvation, and social decay, India is a frightful victim of Hinduism's logical conclusions. If reincarnation is true, then all things are sacred, which is why Hindus do not eat cows, for example, because they are "one" with them. So the people lose the food potential of the cow, while the cow eats food that a human could eat. So there is a double loss. If the cockroach is one with us, or might be related to us, we cannot kill it, so we let it roam free to spread filth and disease.

CONCLUSION

The teachings of the New Age Movement, if taken to their logical extreme, are bad. But that doesn't mean the people who believe them are any worse than the rest of humanity, and it is the responsibility of Christians to share the gospel with them in the hope that they will respond.

Having said that, Christians may not win a strong hearing with New Agers merely by giving them a list of where they are wrong. They are very experience-oriented, and depending on the work of the Holy Spirit in their lives, they may respond better to an approach that recognizes their mind-set. If so, we can invite them to have an experiential encounter with Jesus by giving their lives to Him. We can tell our stories, our experiences as Christians. We can live authentic lives before them. In the beginning, who we are may be more important to them than what we believe. When they have accepted Jesus and are born again, the Holy Spirit within them can guide them into deeper truth.

SPEED BUMP!

Slow down to be sure you've gotten the main points from this chapter.

Q1. What is the New Age Movement?

A1. The New Age Movement is a contemporary spiritual movement that focuses on the restoration of a mystical awareness of humanity's *godlike* potential and ultimate absorption into eternal oneness with the divine.

Q2. What differences does Christianity have with the New Age Movement?

A2. Christianity and the New Age Movement have very little fundamental *agreement.*

Q3. What obstacles interfere with Christians witnessing to followers of the New Age Movement?

A3. Not only religious views, but also basic views on *reality* separate Christianity and the New Age Movement.

Q4. Why would anyone believe Christianity over the New Age Movement?

A4. If one wants his faith to be grounded in *facts,* he will choose Christianity over the New Age Movement.

FILL IN THE BLANK

Q1. What is the New Age Movement?

A1. The New Age Movement is a contemporary spiritual movement that focuses on the restoration of a mystical awareness of humanity's _____ potential and ultimate absorption into eternal oneness with the divine.

Q2. What differences does Christianity have with the New Age Movement?

A2. Christianity and the New Age Movement have very little fundamental

_____.

Q3. What obstacles interfere with Christians witnessing to followers of the New Age Movement?

A3. Not only religious views, but also basic views on _____ separate Christianity and the New Age Movement.

Q4. Why would anyone believe Christianity over the New Age Movement?

A4. If one wants his faith to be grounded in _____, he will choose Christianity over the New Age Movement.

FOR FURTHER THOUGHT AND DISCUSSION

1. What do you think is the major appeal of the New Age Movement for Americans today? Why do you think so many Americans are willing to embrace its beliefs?

2. Even though you may not embrace the New Age Movement as a whole, are there elements of it that appeal to you? Why or why not?

3. What do you think are the most persuasive arguments against New Age beliefs?

WHAT IF I DON'T BELIEVE?

If I don't believe, I will be especially susceptible to allowing New Age thinking to seep into my thinking and values. The values of the New Age Movement are so pervasive throughout American society and culture, from education to politics to religion, that unless I am clear on the differences between the New Age Movement and biblical Christianity, I can easily get duped and also fail to help others safeguard themselves.

FOR FURTHER STUDY

1. Scripture

- Genesis 1:1
- John 1:1–12
- John 14:6
- Hebrews 9:27

2. Books

A Crash Course on the New Age, Elliot Miller
Unmasking the New Age, Douglas Groothuis
Fundamentals of the Faith, Peter Kreeft
*The Gospel and the New Spirituality: Communicating the Truth in a World of
    Spiritual Seekers,* Charles Strohmer

CHAPTER **11**

WHAT IS THE GREAT WAGER?

Granted that faith cannot be proved,
what harm will come to you if you
gamble on its truth and it proves
false? . . . If you gain, you gain all;
if you lose, you lose nothing.
—Blaise Pascal (1623–1662)

Life is uncertain. I remember a number of years ago hearing of a couple in England who were terrified of nuclear war. They had become convinced that it was inevitable. They searched the globe looking for a safe place to live. They studied prevailing winds, upper air currents, water currents, and countries likely to be involved in nuclear war. They finally settled on the Falkland Islands, a remote British crown colony off the coast of Argentina, not far from Antarctica. Not long afterward, in 1982, Argentina asserted its sovereignty over the islands and sent in troops to seize them. In response, England dispatched a large naval task force to retake the islands. After intense naval and air battles, the Argentine military surrendered. Heavy losses were suffered on both sides.

Sometimes you can't win for losing. You travel to one of the most remote locations on earth and still war comes thundering up to your doorstep. In the meantime, the Soviet Union has imploded and thus, with the end of the Cold War, the threat of global nuclear war has been greatly reduced. Life is uncertain.

I read another true story of a lady who learned that her husband had betrayed her, so she decided she would end it all by jumping out of her third-story window. Sometime later she awoke in the hospital to discover that she was still alive. She had landed on her departing husband, who was killed! Life is uncertain.

With the uncertainty of life, we must admit that much of life is a gamble. Sometimes the odds are great, sometimes slim, but almost everything is a calculated risk. I've gambled many times in life. I once sold my house and lived off the equity for nearly a year so that I would have time to write a book, not knowing whether I would be able to find a publisher for it. We all gamble a bit whenever we get on an airplane, and even when we leave our houses in the morning for work, school, or the store. A percentage of people never return but are killed on our streets and highways.

Not only do we gamble *in* life, we gamble *with* life. That is, we are all in some way betting on whether there is a God or whether there is not, and what difference, if any, the answer makes in our life. We have spent the last four chapters explaining why we believe the God of the Bible is superior to any other god a person might worship. Now I would like to turn to the matter of what helps people believe and what hinders them. When I say "believe in," I mean not just intellectual agreement that such a God might exist, but also an agreement to follow Him, to make a personal commitment to Him.

IN THIS CHAPTER WE LEARN THAT . . .

1. Some do not believe in God because they do not want to, and they interpret the evidence accordingly.

2. Some believe in God because they want to, and they interpret the evidence accordingly.

3. The great wager we all make is in staking our lives on whether there is or is not a God.

Do you believe in God? There is enough evidence to believe in God if you want to. And there is enough evidence not to believe in Him if you don't want to. If you look at the evidence with an open mind, I believe you first end up a theist (because of arguments for the existence of God) and then a Christian (because of the evidence for the resurrection). However, if you don't want to believe in God or in the resurrection, you can find evidence to support your desire not to believe. I mentioned earlier the response of Aldous Huxley, the renowned humanist, when asked why he and his friends were so eager to embrace the theory of evolution. He said they desired a liberation from morality, because "morality interfered with our sexual freedom."

If we want to believe in God, we have sufficient evidence to convince ourselves, and we have good company. The same is true if we don't want to believe. So why would someone want to believe or not want to believe? And what is at stake with their wager?

WHY WOULD SOMEONE NOT BELIEVE IN GOD?

Some do not believe in God because they do not want to,
and they interpret the evidence accordingly.

There are a number of reasons why a person might not want to believe in God. Michael Green has written:

> I think of one of the atheists I met who became one overnight through the death of the father whom he idolized. . . . I think of another celebrated atheist, with whom I was due to debate. During the dinner beforehand, it became evident that the cause of her atheism was a series of terrible experiences in a Catholic school as a youngster. Another was a survivor of Auschwitz. Another was brought up in a strongly anti-religious home, and had imbibed his parents' attitude uncritically. . . . We must be people-centered in our approach and discover, if possible, what lies behind the atheist's front. It may of course be sheer reasoning, but I have found that rarely to be the case. (*Evangelism Through the Local Church*, 144–145)

1. Intellectual Opposition

In Green's reflections, there are several reasons given why a person might not want to believe in God, but let's take his last example first. A person may have honest intellectual problems with the decision. This is fairly rare, since few people have given serious, informed thought to God's existence and their responsibility to Him if He does exist. Nevertheless, someone might have genuine intellectual barriers to Christianity, and it might keep him from wanting to commit his life to God. Alister McGrath has written of these intellectual barriers in his book *Intellectuals Don't Need God*, and the following thoughts are drawn largely from his book (64–66).

One intellectual barrier is the belief that Christianity is merely a hangover from the intellectual dark ages. It no longer has a place in the modern world. This is a weak reason. Highly regarded world leaders, intellectuals, scientists, and millions of people who are not ignoramuses find their faith in God completely compatible with the modern world. Nevertheless, this intellectual barrier is a stumbling block for some.

Intellectual barriers keep people from belief in God.

A second barrier is the scientific worldview. Many scientists see the Christian faith as merely a wish fulfillment, unsupported by the facts. I think just the opposite is true. Evolution seems to me to take greater faith than Christianity and is a greater wish fulfillment than Christianity. There are such enormous holes in the theory of evolution that an increasing number of leading scientists are discounting it as a viable explanation for present reality. So, a scientific world is not an overwhelming, unanswerable reason for unbelief, but it is sufficient for some.

A third barrier is that suffering seems incompatible with the idea of a loving God. People complain that a God who is all-powerful and all-loving simply would not let the world go on as it has. He would do something about the pain and suffering. This is, perhaps, the most powerful argument against the existence of God, or if He exists, His worthiness to be worshiped. It is, perhaps, the most common reason why people reject God.

A fourth barrier is the belief that all religions lead to God. People may believe in God, or accept the possibility of God, but they are unwilling to commit to the God of the Bible because they believe that, as long as they are sincere, it doesn't matter. Whatever God you worship, they say, the true God will look at the sincerity and accept it as faith in Him. This is a popular perception.

A final intellectual barrier is that Christianity is based on a series of unjustifiable, outdated, and incredible events that can no longer be taken seriously. The three major offenders are the resurrection, the doctrine of the Incarnation (God taking on the form of human flesh), and the doctrines of sin and salvation.

McGrath spent a chapter on each of these objections, and he summarized his initial response as following:

> Of all the world's religions, it is Christianity that has been subjected to the most intense, persistent, and critical examination over the last three hundred years. It has survived in the most hostile of cultural and intellectual climates. Aggressively secularizing publications—such as *The Myth of God Incarnate* (1977)—often give the impression that something has recently happened to make Christianity unbelievable. The word *modern* is bandied around as if the very word discredited Christianity. But modernity is over. Although this fact has yet to permeate into the darker recesses of the Enlightenment, the Western world has entered into a postmodern situation. And this development has brought exciting new possibilities for Christianity as well as new difficulties. But one thing is clear. The idea that Christianity is obsolete has itself become obsolete. It has a curiously dated feel to it, like a relic of a bygone era. The person who mechanically repeats the parrot cries of earlier generations—"Science has disproved Christianity"; "Christianity is irrelevant in a world come of age"—has become stranded in a time warp. It may take some time for this fact to filter down from the opinion-makers to popular writing, but it has happened. There has been a major shift of ideas. . . . It is a shift in favor of faith. (66)

2. The Failure of Christians or the Church

The failure of individual Christians and the church itself to live up to expectations is a major claim for unbelief. From something as immediate and basic as "all the hypocrites in the church," to revulsion over the Crusades, people are turned off by the church's failures. Add to that the exploitation of parishioners by unscrupulous or inept pastors and priests, the "imperial church," forcing third world spiritual converts also to convert to American ideas of worship, exploitation of primitive converts by missionaries, and televangelists who have fallen morally, and many reject God on those grounds.

It is embarrassing and dreadfully unfortunate that these things happen, but to reject the God of the Bible because they do is not a wise decision. The gospel is rejected, not because of any problems with its inherent credibility, but because of its past or present associations. As a teenager, I recall my older brother declaring that he was no longer going to church because of all the hypocrites in the church. I remember thinking, *Jesus can't be blamed for hypocrites. I'm not going to risk my eternal destiny just because somebody else is doing a bad job of living the Christian life.* I knew plenty of people who were marvelous examples of Christianity. Why didn't the witness of those people lead him to start going to church? I thought it was an insufficient reason, but many people still use it as an excuse.

> **People may reject God because of our bad witness.**

Historical and personal bad examples do not have any necessary or direct bearing on whether a position is true or false. I might have a winsome friend who believes the moon is made of green cheese, and I might have an obnoxious acquaintance who believes it is made of dirt. Neither disposition affects what the moon is made of. Truth in such cases is totally separate from people's beliefs or opinions.

3. The Straw Man Syndrome

Closely related to the above reason is the "straw man" syndrome. People reject what they perceive Christianity to be, not what it really is. They get a misunderstanding or misinterpretation of Christianity and reject it, without understanding what Christianity really is. In fact, Christianity is rarely understood by those who have rejected it. For example, people see television preachers who seem to be motivated by money rather than ministry, and they conclude that all preachers are similarly motivated. Or they hear about extremists who bomb an abortion clinic and conclude that all Christians are social extremists.

4. The Desire for Absolute Certainty

There are those who say, "I won't believe it until you can prove it to me with absolute certainty!" This, of course, is impossible. If we were to say, "I won't believe in Alexander the Great unless you can prove to me with absolute certainty that he existed," you would not believe in Alexander the Great. Absolute certainty on that level is not possible, and we would believe very little if we demanded absolute certainty for all things in life. So this is an unrealistic and inconsistent position, which just a little amount of thought will usually correct.

5. Pride or Inferiority

Some people won't give themselves over to God because of a suffocating sense of inadequacy and inferiority. They say something like, "If God really knew what I am like, He wouldn't want anything to do with me!" This is often said quite sincerely and with great anguish. There are two points in response. First, God already knows what we are like. He created us and knows all things (Psalm 139:1–6). Second, the very reason Jesus came was to save sinners (Mark 2:17). Admitting that you are a terrible sinner or insignificant person does not keep you from being saved. It is a condition in order to be saved!

Pride and feelings of inferiority keep people from belief.

On the other hand, there are those who are unwilling to admit that they need to be saved. This looks like pride, but it is probably a desperate attempt to wrap themselves up with self-generated worth. Their sense of inferiority, insecurity, and inadequacy will not allow them to admit to themselves or anyone else that they are in need of saving.

6. Carnality

There are those who are unwilling to give their lives to God because they don't want to stop sinning. It's as simple as that. As long as they can claim that God doesn't exist, or that He doesn't condemn people for sins, or that there is no sin, they will do so in order to justify and hold on to their current lifestyles.

So the question boils down to whether you would like to believe in God and whether you would like to become a Christian. If you would, you have ample evidence and good company.

WHY WOULD SOMEONE WANT TO BELIEVE IN GOD?

Some believe in God because they want to, and they interpret the evidence accordingly.

People are inclined to believe in God for a number of reasons.

1. To Escape Hell

Humans often do not have a well-developed capacity to appreciate God's values. The highest reason for believing in and serving God is to bring glory to Him. Yet the lowest reason, avoiding punishment, is often easiest to understand and the most compelling. For this reason, a desire to escape eternal punishment is a common reason people decide to believe in God. Jesus used it throughout the Gospels as a motive for repentance. I remember well when I became a Christian as a young college student; my primary motivation was fear of what would happen to me when I died.

A belief in hell is waning in American society, and therefore fear of hell is diminishing as a motivational factor in commitment to Christianity. Back in the infancy of our nation, Jonathan Edwards preached a sermon entitled "Sinners in the Hands of an Angry God." In it, he graphically detailed the horror of hell and the thin thread of life that is holding most people out of hell. It is said that men groaned in fear and women swooned at this sermon, which was partially responsible for starting a great spiritual awakening. Today, if that sermon were preached, people would be more likely to yawn or snicker. The times have changed. Yet there are those, like myself, who find this still to be a compelling reason to believe in God.

2. Hope of Heaven

This is the flip-side of the fear of hell. People are motivated to believe in God because they want heaven. They want an eternity of bliss, a wonderful life without pain, heartache, and tears. People who have suffered terribly in this world often long for heaven. People with broken bodies or chronic illnesses long for a place where their bodies will be whole. People with broken relationships or lost loved ones long for heaven where relationships will be whole. Many slaves before the Civil War had a highly developed sense of heaven, since their life on earth was so miserable. Heaven was the only thing they had to look forward to. Sometimes it is more the hope of heaven than the fear of hell that motivates people to believe in God.

3. Intuitive Belief

Many people believe in God because, when they look at the starry heavens, something deep within them cries out, "There must be a God." When they look at the ocean, or witness the birth of a baby, or ponder the intricacies of nature, something cries out in them, "There must be a God." All that they see around them, evolutionary scientists notwithstanding, does not seem to be explained by anything less than a supreme Creator-God.

Others search their inner thoughts for an explanation of where we came from, why we are here, and where we are going, and nothing satisfies them as much as the answer that there is a supreme Creator-God. There is something unique about humanity—a longing for God, a desire for eternity—that seems to come from within. For many, there is an intuitive sense that there is a God.

WHY I NEED TO KNOW THIS

I need to know this so that I can have confidence in the existence of God. If I understand that the primary reason many people do not believe in God is because they do not want to, rather than because the evidence demands unbelief, then I can have greater confidence in the reasonableness of my own faith. In addition, I can find more effective ways of helping others consider the reasonableness of believing in God.

4. Purpose and Meaning

Others see no purpose or meaning in life unless there is God. If we are just the result of a biological accident, then life has no meaning because we are of no more inherent worth than a rock or a cactus. We are alone in the universe. Even if there are other beings in the universe somewhere, we are all biological accidents. We are cosmic orphans. We are alone, and there is no ultimate meaning in life, no reason to keep going.

5. Credibility of the Bible

The Bible is a remarkable book. It records prophecies that were given years, decades, and centuries before they were fulfilled. It gives a plausible explanation for the world as we know it. It has a keen understanding of the nature of humanity. It contains wisdom so startling, so far above anything written anywhere else, that it seems to be a unique book. It speaks to our hearts, it explains our conditions, it warns us of harmful behavior and encourages us to helpful behavior. When we obey it we prosper; when we violate it we suffer, whether on a personal or national level. It is a towering book, unlike any other, and for many, it provides a compelling reason to believe in God.

6. The Life of Jesus

Jesus is the most important person ever to have lived. There is not another person in all of history who has had nearly the impact on the world that Jesus has. His teachings are so profound, His life so exemplary, and His works so remarkable, that He is a compelling figure. Many people want to believe in God because of the life of Jesus.

Not only His life, but also His death and resurrection are compelling. If you apply equally the same criteria to the resurrection that you apply to any other historical event, you must come away saying the resurrection happened. Only if a person had a reason for not wanting to believe the resurrection would he deny it.

Jesus' life, death, and resurrection are so compelling that many people believe in God because of them.

WHAT IS THE GREAT WAGER?

The great wager we all make is in staking our lives on whether there is or is not a God.

These, then, are some of the reasons why a person might believe or not believe in God. But what causes a person to go one way or the other? To begin analyzing this question, let's return to the issue with which we began, that life is fraught with calculated risks. With some of the risks, there is nothing to lose and much to gain. For example, suppose you were dying of an incurable disease and the doctors said that you would die shortly. Then news came from a research hospital that a drug had been developed that might save your life. They did not know for sure, but there was a 50/50 chance that it would work and you would live. Wouldn't you try it? You would have everything to gain and nothing to lose.

In a slightly different scenario, imagine that, by subscribing to a magazine, the publisher gave you one of two sweepstakes tickets, and that one of these was the winning ticket—to a new house, a new car, a million dollars! Would you not buy the subscription? You might not win anything, but you would have little to lose if you did not win.

Most people would not hesitate to "gamble" in either situation. In one you had everything to win, and in the other you had little to lose. Since we see the wisdom of "betting" in these kinds of cases, would it not make sense to "bet" on God, even if you have no proof, no guarantee that He exists?

People ought to gamble their lives with God.

This idea of wagering a life on God is found in the writings of Blaise Pascal, a seventeenth-century French mathematician, scientist, and philosopher. In his classic writing *Pensees* (*Thoughts*), he wrote that either God is or He is not, but that you cannot prove God or disprove Him, so on what basis do we believe in Him? He encouraged people to "wager" with their lives. That is, he encouraged people to "bet" that God existed and to live accordingly, rather than to "bet" that He didn't exist and live accordingly. His argument had the following three points:

1. We do not have the option of not wagering. If we do not wager that God exists, then, by default, we are wagering that He does not. Since we are all going to die, and since, if God exists, we must answer to Him for our lives, we automatically wager against Him unless we wager in favor of Him.

2. If we wager that God exists, and we are right, we win everything. We win a meaningful, purposeful life on earth and eternal happiness in heaven. If we wager that God exists and we are wrong, we have lost little, perhaps nothing.

3. If we wager that God does not exist and we are right, we have gained little. The life of an unbeliever is no richer on earth than the life of a believer. Often, it can seem much worse because of a sense of emptiness. But if we wager that God does not exist and we are wrong, then we face eternal destruction in hell.

Does it not make sense, then, that the safest position is to wager your life on the belief that God exists, and to follow Him in faith? There is everything to gain if you do and everything to lose if you don't.

There is plenty of information to believe if you want to. No one has to commit intellectual suicide by believing in God. Most, if not all, of the presidents of the United States have professed belief in God. Many of the world's greatest scientists, statesmen, educators, artists, and humanitarians have been Christians. Why not take a reasonable way that is safe?

Pascal then suggested what a person should do if he wants to believe but can't. He wrote that if your head (intellect) tells you to believe, but your heart (faith) is unwilling to go along, it is because of your desires, since reason compels you to believe. So he suggests that you diminish your desires rather than amass additional intellectual reasons to believe. If you want to find faith but don't know the way, if you want to be cured of unbelief but don't know how, then learn from those who have faith. Simply begin acting as if you did believe. Begin living a good life and attend worship services. As you do, your faith will grow. You can "act" your way into "believing."

This "acting" approach might not work for everyone, so let me add another suggestion: ask God for faith. We see an example of such a request in Mark 9:20–24, when an anguished father brought his son to Jesus and asked Him to heal him from demon possession. Jesus said, "If you can believe, all things are possible to him who believes." The father cried out, "Lord, I believe; help my unbelief!"

People can pray to receive more faith.

If someone knelt and prayed to Jesus, saying, "Lord, my head tells me it is reasonable to believe in You, but I just don't seem to be moved to do it, so help me place my faith in You," I have to believe that God would honor that prayer. In the Gospel of John, Jesus said, "The one who comes to Me I will by no means cast out" (6:37). If anyone came to Jesus with this prayer, He would not turn him away.

CONCLUSION

In his book *Fundamentals of the Faith*, Peter Kreeft wrote about the time in which Pascal lived:

> Pascal lived during a time of great skepticism. Medieval philosophy was dead, and medieval theology was being ignored or sneered at by the new intellectuals of the scientific revolution of the seventeenth century. Montaigne, the great skeptical essayist, was the most popular writer of the day. The classic arguments for the existence of God were no longer popularly believed. What could the Christian apologist [one who defends the faith] say to the skeptical mind of this age? Suppose such a typical mind lacked both the gift of faith and the confidence in reason to prove God's existence; could there be a third ladder out of the pit of unbelief into the light of belief?
>
> Pascal's Wager claims to be that third ladder. (49)

Is not our day similar to Pascal's day? Is this not a day of great skepticism? Is not biblical theology being largely ignored? Are not the classical arguments for the existence of God often doubted? Does not the wager make as much sense today as it did in Pascal's day?

SPEED BUMP!

Slow down to be sure you've gotten the main points from this chapter.

Q1. Why would someone not believe in God?

A1. Some do not believe in God because they do *not* want to, and they interpret the evidence accordingly.

Q2. Why would someone want to believe in God?

A2. Some believe in God because they *want* to, and they interpret the evidence accordingly.

Q3. What is the great wager?

A3. The great wager we all make is in *staking* our lives on whether there is or is not a God.

FILL IN THE BLANKS

Q1. Why would someone not believe in God?

A1. Some do not believe in God because they do _____ want to, and they interpret the evidence accordingly.

Q2. Why would someone want to believe in God?

A2. Some believe in God because they _____ to, and they interpret the evidence accordingly.

Q3. What is the great wager?

A3. The great wager we all make is in _____ our lives on whether there is or is not a God.

FOR FURTHER THOUGHT AND DISCUSSION

1. Do you, by nature, want to believe in God or not want to believe in Him? Are your reasons the same as some listed in this chapter, or are there others?

2. What, to you, is the most compelling reason to believe in God?

3. Does the wager seem reasonable to you? Have you "bet" your life on God? Why or why not?

WHAT IF I DON'T BELIEVE?

If I don't believe in the reasonableness of the wager, I might decide to reject God, either directly, by conscious rejection, or indirectly, by just neglecting to accept Him. Unless I am brought to see that I cannot avoid wagering my life on God, I might put off the wager, thinking I had time, but then eventually running out of time, as we all do.

FOR FURTHER STUDY

1. Scripture

- John 3:16–18
- Hebrews 11:1
- Hebrews 11:6

2. Books

Fundamentals of the Faith, Peter Kreeft
Making Sense of It All, Thomas V. Morris

CHAPTER **12**

HOW DO I TELL MY STORY?

*Spiritual truth is discernible only to
a pure heart, not to a keen intellect.
It is not a question of profundity
of intellect, but purity of heart.*
—**Oswald Chambers (1874–1917)**

I have sat through many sermons in my life. I attended a Christian college for four years where we had chapel every day. I also went to church twice on Sunday and once in the middle of the week. Then, I went to seminary where I did the same for another four years. After that, I taught at a Christian college for a number of years where I also heard many sermons. I wish I could say that I am a good sermon listener as a result, but I am not. I find it difficult to keep my mind from wandering. Occasionally, my wife, who is a good sermon listener, will ask me what the preacher said, or what he meant, or what passage he was taking us to, and I am often chagrined to admit that, mentally, I was wandering out in the ozone somewhere.

I am embarrassed by this weakness and do not mention it with satisfaction. But I know that I am not alone, so I have tried to study what kind of preaching "holds" me, in order to learn to help hold the ones to whom I preach. I remember a particular struggle one Sunday, when I drifted out into the stratosphere after just a few minutes into the sermon. When the preacher told a story, I came back. Not long after he finished his story, I drifted again. Then, he told another story and I came back, and I learned to appreciate those stories dearly.

That made me wonder how people were reacting to me when I preached. I wondered if they, too, were drifting in and out. It occurred to me that if, when people left mentally, they also left physically, it would have a dramatic effect on our preaching. I imagined myself preaching, and suddenly, Ken was gone—Ken, my good friend! How could he do that? But he wasn't gone long. He soon came

> **The power of
> a story can
> be a dramatic
> witness.**

IN THIS CHAPTER WE LEARN THAT . . .

1. We need to tell stories to accommodate how people listen and learn.

2. We should tell our story of how we accepted God's story (the gospel).

3. We must validate our story with personal integrity.

back. Probably just went out to check out the golf course. Oh—Barbara just slipped out. She's probably worrying about her newborn in the nursery. Ol' Bill checked out shortly after I began and didn't return until I said "Amen" at the end. Ingrate! See if I come running the next time he wants something from me!

If that happened to me just one Sunday, I know I would never be the same. It would drive me to heretofore unknown levels of commitment to be interesting and relevant. So one of the things I try to do when I am preparing a sermon is to "listen" to it in my mind when I have finished, to see where I think people are likely to leave the room. Then I try to put something in the text to help people stay in the room. One of the most helpful things to keep people in the room is a good story. When we tell good ones, people stick around. When we go too long without one, we often lose them.

Jesus told stories all the time during His ministry. In Matthew 13:34, the apostle wrote, "And all these things Jesus spoke to the multitude in parables; and without a parable He did not speak to them." A parable is a story. If He told stories, could it be wrong for me to tell them?

The power of a story is dramatic almost wherever it is told. In this final chapter, we want to look at the value of a story in sharing the gospel with others.

WHY DO WE NEED TO TELL STORIES?

We need to tell stories to accommodate how people listen and learn.

There are several reasons why storytelling is an important and helpful medium for communicating spiritual truth. We want to investigate these reasons in this section of the chapter.

Attention Span

One reason to tell stories is because of a shortened national attention span. Because of television and other visual influences, many of us do not read well or concentrate well, and we have a shortened ability to keep our minds focused on things. Instead of hard mental work, people want to be entertained by visual images. In a deeply insightful book I read sometime back, *Amusing Ourselves to Death*, Neil Postman observed that we have transitioned from an age of exposition to an age of entertainment. Previous generations were "reading" generations, and those who wrote good books were the superstars of the day.

People who can read are able to focus their attention for long periods of time; they can sit through long speeches, lectures, and teachings, holding thoughts in their minds, on which other thoughts are developed, and then wait until the end to tie the knot of complete understanding. When Abraham Lincoln debated Stephen Douglas over the issue of slavery, the debates often lasted for six to seven hours.

Today, we have trouble holding our attention span on anything for six to seven minutes, let alone difficult matters. Because of television, I believe we have succumbed to needing our information to be condensed, predigested, and accompanied by visuals. We are more and more dependent on the people who can package the information well enough to spoon-feed us with it. The result is a stunted ability to comprehend important information.

Examples of this tendency are apparent in the national presidential campaigns. During the 1992 campaign, the television news networks were criticized for reducing the national political debate to a series of nightly seven- to eight-second sound bites. Responding to the criticism, CBS News announced that it was going to increase its coverage from eight seconds to twenty-four seconds (as if that would solve the problem)!

We are tempted to criticize the media for this, but the media are simply responding to reality. If one network has seven-second sound bites, and another has seven-minute segments, and everyone watches the seven-second network, then the other network cannot long afford to produce seven-minute segments. It is all money-driven and based on the appetites of the public. If the public would accept longer news segments, the networks would provide them. So the problem is deeper than merely television.

WHY I NEED TO KNOW THIS

I need to know this so that I will defend my faith in a way that means something to the people I am talking with. If I understand the power of story, I can put the truth in a form that is understood and often accepted.

We in the church are not exempt from these problems. Let's be careful at whom we cast stones; we might be guilty of the same thing ourselves. Are we in the church moving into a period in which we are trivializing the gospel? Postman has suggested that we in the church have turned the Christian faith into just another form of entertainment. Christian books, Christian television, and even church worship services have in some cases fallen in step with the larger entertainment industry. The goal in some Christian organizations, endeavors, and churches is to hold an audience long enough to make a profit.

On one level, you cannot ignore audience and profit. A church cannot survive if it cannot pay its bills. But trivializing the gospel and becoming an ecclesiastical entertainment industry is not the answer.

Leighton Ford, in his book *The Power of Story*, has written:

> All too often, in our attempts to "sell" the gospel as a television show or a product in a Christian bookstore, we have watered down the truth of the Story of God. And this we must never do. Instead we must find a bridge between entertainment and exposition, between what people want to see and what people desperately need to hear. I am convinced that the bridge between entertainment and exposition is narrative, the act of storytelling.

Of course, we cannot do without exposition, but our exposition must be laced with sufficient narrative and story to hold the shortened attention spans of those we hope to reach.

Cultural Shift

A second reason we can use storytelling with effectiveness is because of the current dramatic cultural shift. Each generation tends to bring a different set of values to culture. Children of the Great Depression era are different from World War II children, who are different from baby boomers, who are different from baby busters, Gen Xers, Gen Nexters, and so on with each succeeding generation. The older generations often do not like, or identify with, many of the values of the younger generations.

Younger generations used to be annoying to older generations. Now the generational differences are occurring so rapidly, and are so stark and alarming, that younger generations are almost frightening to older generations.

Confronted with such rapid and stark generational changes, we can see that the way of evangelizing and equipping Christians that worked with one generation may not work with another. If we are going to reach succeeding generations for

Christ, we will need to "read" the culture, as we would if we went overseas as missionaries, and reach them in culturally relevant ways. The apostle Paul approached Gentiles differently than he approached Jews (1 Corinthians 1:23). We will have to do the same with differing generations. Using story, however, may become more important with succeeding generations, rather than less.

The power of story is particularly important today, and is likely to remain so, because of how younger generations now perceive truth. There has been a shift from older generations who embraced absolute truth to younger generations who do not. So, when we attempt to share the gospel or defend our faith with younger generations, many people are uninfluenced by statements of objective truth. Further, unchurched people may become suspicious and defensive when we get too dogmatic in our statements.

Rather than give them a list of objective reasons for believing in Jesus, we can tell a story of how we came to believe in Jesus. The story can incorporate the list of objective reasons. In doing so, we have told them the reasons, but in a way that is less intimidating to them (because they are not being forced to agree or disagree with us regarding the truth of the reasons), and they cannot deny that those reasons persuaded us. If we merely gave them the list and told them they ought to be persuaded by it, they could say, "Oh no, we oughtn't!" And, since people's experiences are usually respected by others, stories are an acceptable form to them.

WHAT STORY SHOULD WE TELL?

We should tell our story of how we accepted God's story (the gospel).

God's story, in its most basic form, is simple:

1. God created humanity to live in perfect fellowship and harmony with God forever in paradise (Genesis 1—3).

2. Humanity rebelled against God in the Garden of Eden (Genesis 3).

3. Sin entered the world at that time and humanity became separated from God, spiritually dead, and lost without hope (Ephesians 2:1–14).

4. God loved us and sent His Son, Jesus Christ, to die for our sins, that if we repent of our sin and believe in Jesus, God will forgive our sins and impute Jesus' righteousness to us (Romans 5:1–21; 2 Corinthians 5:21).

5. When this happens, we are forgiven and spiritually born again, destined for heaven when we die (John 3:16).

6. We will live in heaven with God in perfect righteousness and fellowship forever (Romans 6:23).

There is much more that could be added to the story, but nothing from the
foregoing should be omitted. When we talk to others, we should be sure to focus on
the fact that God loves us, that Jesus died for our sins, and that we can be forgiven
and made new. If we focus on the story of God's love for us, we may get a greater
hearing for the meaning and purpose that this life has, and for the hope of eternal
life.

We must tell *our* story, which is the story of how God's life and our life inter-
sected. We can tell the story of how we came to realize that we were sinners,
separated from God and without hope. We can tell people how, and under what
circumstances, we came to believe that we were sinners, that we believed that Jesus
is the Son of God, and that we repented of our sin and gave our life to Jesus. We

can tell them the changes that have happened in our lives since
we made the decision to believe in Jesus. We can tell them the
hope we have for eternal life with God when we die. Simply put,
we just tell them the story of our salvation.

**People cannot
dispute our
stories.**

My story is that I grew up in a good moral home, although
it was not an overtly Christian home. All we knew was what we
learned in church, and all we learned in church were Bible stories
and good morals. We were never told the way of salvation, so we
lived in the light we had. I was a good kid in high school, but when I went to college,
without a true Christian "center" to my life, I began to live like the devil. I became
filled with remorse over the things I was doing, and as a result I felt trapped—not
wanting to sin, but feeling helpless to stop. On Sunday morning, I told myself I
was never going to do "that stuff" anymore, but the next Saturday night, I did it
anyway.

My behavior made me feel terribly guilty, and I began to fear death. I figured
that if heaven was a perfect place, I couldn't go there because I wasn't perfect. And
I had no idea how to become perfect. The guilt and the fear began to make my life
miserable. I had no purpose for living, no reason to stay in college, no meaning in
anything I did.

One evening, the summer after my first year in college, I was back in my small
hometown playing basketball in the city park with a high school friend. He was a
Christian, and we got onto the subject of religion. He told me God's story, and that
night I committed my life to Christ. I was concerned about turning over a new leaf,
because I had done that before, but the leaf always turned back over again. This

time, my friend said, things would be different; the Holy Spirit would come to live inside me and help me become the person God wanted me to be.

The years that have followed since then have proved him right. It was not merely a matter of turning over another new leaf. The power of God was in me, not to live a perfect life but to live a growing, godly life and not give up trying. I now have a purpose and meaning in life that is quite rewarding, and I no longer fear death. I look forward to heaven, when we can all live in perfect fellowship with God and with each other, unhindered by sin.

When we tell people our story, they may not agree with our decisions, conclusions, and actions, but it is unlikely they will dispute that it is our story. And within the story is the seed of the gospel, which the Holy Spirit can use to draw them to Jesus.

If you debate them on the reasons why people should believe the resurrection, they can reject the reasons. But if you tell them that you believe the resurrection for such and such reasons, they cannot say, "Oh, no, you don't." There is nothing for them to do but listen, because you are telling it as your story. And it may give them hope that it can become their story too.

When those of us over forty look at young people dressed in black with earrings, nose rings, lip rings, baggy clothes, and oddly cut hair, we may be tempted to believe that they are beyond hope. But they are not. They have the same fundamental longings that we do, the same needs that Jesus will meet, and many of them will be in heaven. We need to put ourselves in their shoes. We need to realize that if we had been born in their circumstances instead of the ones we were born into, we might be like them instead of how we are. And we need to do unto them as we would have them do unto us, if we were in their shoes. One of the things we can do is tell them the story of God and our own story, and then pray for them that it may become their story.

HOW MUST WE VALIDATE OUR STORY?

We must validate our story with personal integrity.

Christians ought to be the number-one best advertisement for Christianity, but often they are not. In his book *Following Christ*, Joe Stowell has written:

> Living in Chicago, I am aware of what graffiti can do to an otherwise attractive facade. Throughout history, vandals have destroyed masterpieces of art by wanton strokes of a brush, adding glasses, a mustache, a sinister smile, a beard, or a distorted nose.

Too often we have graffitied the face of Christ. His image becomes clouded by our prejudices and preferences. Apart from our activities on Sunday and our conformity to external codes of dos and don'ts, the world doesn't notice much difference between us and people who don't claim to be Christians. All they see in Christianity is the loss of a day of leisure on the weekend and the denial of common pleasures. Nor does it go unnoticed that many professing Christians manifest as much greed, self-centeredness, materialism, anger, aggressiveness, and sensualism as the average pagan on the street. (11)

This is not the way it is supposed to be. People are supposed to be drawn to Jesus because of what they see of Him in us. Jesus Himself said in John 13:34–35, "A new commandment I give to you, that you love one another; as I have loved you, that you also love one another. By this all will know that you are My disciples, if you have love for one another."

The love Jesus is talking about is not the slobbery sentimentalism and hailstorm of emotions that pass as love today. Rather, this is a self-sacrificing love that directs itself toward the good of others. It is described well by the apostle Paul in 1 Corinthians 13:4–7:

> Love is patient, love is kind. It does not envy, it does not boast, it is not proud. It is not rude, it is not self-seeking, it is not easily angered, it keeps no record of wrongs. Love does not delight in evil but rejoices with the truth. It always protects, always trusts, always hopes, always perseveres. (NIV)

That is the kind of love Jesus is calling us to. Jesus said that when Christians manifest that kind of love to one another, the world will conclude that we are authentic disciples of Christ. If we do not manifest that kind of love to one another, the world will have a reason to conclude that we are hypocrites, a conclusion that is widely held today.

In another passage, Jesus again mentioned the profound power of love. In John 17:20–21, He said in a prayer, "I pray . . . that all of them [His followers] may be one, Father, just as you are in me and I am in you. May they also be in us so that the world may believe that you have sent me" (NIV).

From this passage, we learn another startling truth. The unity that Jesus prayed for can only be produced by mutual love, such as we saw in the 1 Corinthians 13 passage. If we love one another with that kind of love, it produces unity, and the unity persuades the watching world that Jesus has been sent by God. If the world does not see that kind of unity produced by love, then they have a reason to conclude that Jesus was not sent by God. They would be wrong, but they would still have a good complaint. Francis Schaeffer developed this point clearly in his marvelous little book *The Mark of the Christian.*

So in summary, Schaeffer makes the points that when we fail to love one another, the world has a reason to conclude that we are not true disciples (we are hypocrites) and that Jesus was not sent from God (He was just a man). By and large, these are two of the most formidable conclusions thrown back to us by the world.

When we tell our story without backing it up with authentic Christlike character, the story is diluted, washed-out, and anemic. It has a fraction of the impact it should. But when we tell our story with the strength of an authentic Christlike character, the story is strengthened and made powerful.

One day, the unity of the church will be a powerful story.

I remember sharing my story, a little at a time over a period of a number of months, with an unchurched psychologist with whom I was working. He did not accept Jesus at that time, but he was impressed with the reasonableness of authentic Christianity. We were talking about the faith one day, sitting in a restaurant, when he said quite hotly, "Why is it that you call yourself a Christian and all those spiritual quacks I see on TV also call themselves Christians? You're not the same at all. There ought to be two different names for you."

I certainly don't want to affirm his generalization that all Christians on TV are spiritual quacks. What I want to say is that he had not rejected Jesus. He had rejected a straw man that some Christians had helped construct. We cannot control whether others validate their story with integrity—with authentic Christian character—and none of us will represent Jesus flawlessly. But we must be intent on validating our story with integrity and with honest and growing, albeit imperfect, authenticity.

CONCLUSION

The newer generation of people, whom we are commissioned by God to reach for Christ, must often be reached in ways different than past generations were reached. Many today don't believe in absolute truth, so presenting verifiable, logical information, which has worked in the past, does not always work with them. Leighton Ford's son, Kevin, has written that the church will have to change the way it communicates. The new generation relates to communication forms that are functional and minimalist. When we speak to them we must keep it clean and simple, nouns and verbs, not a lot of adverbs and adjectives. We must give them pictures, graphics, color, motion, sound. Above all, if we want to make a point, we must not give them a lot of dry content. We must tell them a story (Ford, 48).

We don't change the ultimate goal of Christlikeness. We don't lower the top of the ladder. But we may need to add some rungs to the bottom, to help people get the foothold they need. We can wish it weren't necessary, and we can lament the loss of absolute truth and mental concentration. Or we can accept that that's the way it is and find ways to reach them, as well as to defend our faith, with a story.

SPEED BUMP!

Slow down to be sure you've gotten the main points from this chapter.

Q1. Why do we need to tell stories?

A1. We need to tell stories to accommodate how people *listen* and *learn*.

Q2. What story should we tell?

A2. We should tell our story of how we *accepted* God's story (the gospel).

Q3. How must we validate our story?

A3. We must validate our story with personal *integrity*.

FILL IN THE BLANK

Q1. Why do we need to tell stories?

A1. We need to tell stories to accommodate how people _____ and _____.

Q2. What story should we tell?

A2. We should tell our story of how we _____ God's story (the gospel).

Q3. How must we validate our story?

A3. We must validate our story with personal _____.

FOR FURTHER THOUGHT AND DISCUSSION

1. Are you part of the newer generation or part of the older? Which of the general values of your generation do you think are good? Which ones are bad? How do you view those of the other generation? What do you think your response

should be to them? How can you use your place in history to best further the kingdom of God?

2. Have you ever studied God's story enough so that you could tell it briefly from memory? If you have not, would you be willing to? Study how the story is summarized in this chapter to help you.

3. Have you ever thought through your own story to the point that you could share it with someone? If not, would you be willing to? See if you can write your story down in about the same number of words that I used in writing mine in this chapter.

WHAT IF I DON'T BELIEVE?

If I don't believe in the importance of stories, I may miss many opportunities to influence others for the cause of Christ, and I may fail in my responsibility to be able to defend my faith (1 Peter 3:15).

FOR FURTHER STUDY

1. Scripture

- Genesis 1–3
- Matthew 13:34
- John 3:16
- Romans 5:1–21
- Romans 6:23
- 2 Corinthians 5:21
- Ephesians 2:1–14
- 1 Peter 3:15

2. Books

The Power of Story, Leighton Ford
Amusing Ourselves to Death, Neil Postman
Following Christ, Joe Stowell
The Mark of the Christian, Francis Schaeffer

BIBLIOGRAPHY

Beverley, James. *Christ and Islam*. Joplin, MO: College Press, 1997.

Ford, Leighton. *The Power of Story*. Colorado Springs: NavPress, 1994.

Geisler, Norman L. and Abdul Saleeb. *Answering Islam*. Grand Rapids: Baker Books, 1993.

Green, Michael. *My God*. Nashville: Thomas Nelson Publishers, 1993.

Green, Michael. *Who Is This Jesus?* Nashville: Thomas Nelson Publishers, 1992.

Green, Michael and Alister McGrath. *How Shall We Reach Them?* Nashville: Thomas Nelson Publishers, 1995.

Groothuis, Douglas. *Unmasking the New Age*. Downers Grove, IL: InterVarsity Press, 1986.

Kennedy, D. James. *What If Jesus Had Never Been Born?* Nashville: Thomas Nelson Publishers, 1994.

Kreeft, Peter. *Fundamentals of the Faith*. San Francisco: Ignatius Press, 1988.

Lewis, C. S. *A Grief Observed*. New York: Seabury Press, 1961.

Lewis, C. S. *Mere Christianity*. New York: Macmillan, 1960.

Lewis, C. S. *The Problem of Pain*. New York: Macmillan, 1961.

McDowell, Josh. *Answers to Tough Questions*. San Bernardino, CA: Here's Life Publishers, 1980; reprint, Nashville: Thomas Nelson Publishers.

McDowell, Josh. *Evidence That Demands a Verdict*. San Bernardino, CA: Here's Life Publishers, 1979; reprint, Nashville: Thomas Nelson Publishers.

Miller, Elliot. *A Crash Course on the New Age*. Grand Rapids: Baker Book House, 1989.

Morris, Thomas V. *Making Sense of It All*. Grand Rapids: Wm. B. Eerdmans, 1992.

Pinnock, Clark. *Set Forth Your Case*. Chicago: Moody Press, 1971.

Postman, Neil. *Amusing Ourselves to Death*. New York: Penguin Books, 1986.

Schaeffer, Francis. *The Church at the End of the Twentieth Century*. Downers Grove, IL: InterVarsity Press, 1970.

Story, Dan. *Defending Your Faith*. Nashville: Thomas Nelson Publishers, 1992.

Stowell, Joseph M. *Following Christ*. Grand Rapids: Zondervan, 1995.

Strohmer, Charles. *The Gospel and the New Spirituality: Communicating the Truth in a World of Spiritual Seekers*. Nashville: Oliver Nelson, 1996.

Yancey, Philip. *Open Windows*. Westchester, IL: Crossway Books, 1982.

Yancey, Philip. *The Jesus I Never Knew*. Grand Rapids: Zondervan, 1996.

Zacharias, Ravi. *Can Man Live Without God?* Dallas: Word Publishing, 1994.

MASTER REVIEW

Chapter 1

Q1. What is the contemporary crisis over truth?

A1. The contemporary crisis concerns whether or not *objective truth* exists and how well people can know it.

Q2. How does the Bible view truth?

A2. The Bible views truth as *objective*, coming from God Himself, and something that can be known, as fully as God permits.

Q3. How can we present and defend the truth effectively?

A3. We combine a credible *lifestyle* with an appropriate presentation of truth.

Q4. Why do people deny the existence of truth?

A4. Many people deny the existence of truth and ignore the gospel because they do not want to be *accountable* to it.

Chapter 2

Q1. Why would someone not believe in God?

A1. Some people reject God because the world is *inconsistent* with their concept of God.

Q2. Why would someone believe in God?

A2. People accept God because the existence of God is the best *explanation* for the world as it is.

Q3. What is the role of the will in deciding about God?

A3. We often believe what we want to believe regardless of the *evidence*.

Chapter 3

Q1. Does the Bible claim that Jesus was God?

A1. The Bible makes *clear* that Jesus was God.

Q2. Did Jesus fulfill prophecy?

A2. Jesus *fulfilled* all prophecies necessary to qualify as the Messiah.

Q3. Did Jesus speak divine words?

A3. The words that Jesus spoke went *beyond* the words of a mere man, and were divine.

Q4. Did Jesus do divine deeds?

A4. The deeds that Jesus did went *beyond* the deeds of a mere man, and were divine.

Q5. Did Jesus rise from the dead?

A5. Both the Bible and history *confirm* that Jesus rose from the dead.

Chapter 4

Q1. What claim does the Bible make for itself?

A1. The Bible claims to be the Word of God, without *error*.

Q2. Why do we believe the Bible is reliable?

A2. Ancient manuscripts, archaeology, and prophecy all *support* the reliability of the Bible.

Q3. How does the Bible describe the human condition?

A3. The Bible accurately describes humanity as inherently *flawed* and without ability to correct itself.

Q4. How has the Bible influenced humanity?

A4. The Bible has had a *positive* influence on humanity wherever it has been known and followed.

Chapter 5

Q1. Why would anyone say that Jesus is the only way to God?

A1. We can say Jesus is the only way to God because the *Bible* says He is the only way.

Q2. Can people who have never heard of Jesus be saved?

A2. The Christian community is increasingly *divided* on whether or not a person can be saved without having heard of Jesus.

Q3. What about those who cannot understand the gospel?

A3. There is a general *consensus* that those who cannot understand the gospel will be saved.

Chapter 6

Q1. Where did evil come from?

A1. Evil originated with *Satan* and entered the world with Adam and Eve.

Q2. Why doesn't God remove evil?

A2. God cannot destroy all evil without destroying *humanity*.

Q3. How can God be good and still allow evil and suffering?

A3. An infinite, holy God has thoughts and ways that are *higher* than ours.

Q4. What good can come of evil and suffering?

A4. Evil and suffering are not good, but God can *use* them for good.

Chapter 7

Q1. What is Judaism?

A1. Judaism believes that true worship is of *Jehovah* (Yahweh) only, not Jesus Christ.

Q2. What differences does Christianity have with Judaism?

A2. The primary difference Christianity has with Judaism is that Jews do not accept Jesus as the *Messiah*.

Q3. What obstacles interfere with Christians witnessing to Jews?

A3. Widely differing opinions on the need for *atonement* and the nature of the coming *Messiah* are formidable obstacles for Christians in witnessing to Jews.

Q4. Why would anyone believe Christianity over Judaism?

A4. If Jesus is who He said He was, then one would *choose* Christianity over Judaism.

Chapter 8

Q1. What is Islam?

A1. Islam, based on the teachings of the prophet *Muhammad*, claims to worship the same God as Judaism and Christianity (the God of Abraham) but does not believe in essential Christian doctrines.

Q2. What difference does Christianity have with Islam?

A2. The primary difference Christianity has with Islam is that Muslims do not accept *Jesus* as the Son of God.

Q3. What obstacles interfere with Christians witnessing to Muslims?

A3. Widely differing opinions on *Jesus* and the *Bible* are formidable obstacles for Christians witnessing to Muslims.

Q4. Why would anyone believe Christianity rather than Islam?

A4. The gospel story of God's love in *Jesus*, proven by His miracles, teaching, sacrificial life and death, and glorious resurrection, outshines the message of Islam, which knows little of the love of God and a personal relationship with Him.

Chapter 9

Q1. What are Eastern religions?

A1. Eastern religions originated in *Asia* and commonly believe in karma, reincarnation, and nirvana.

Q2. What differences does Christianity have with Eastern religions?

A2. Christianity and Eastern religions see very little in *common*.

Q3. What obstacles interfere with Christians witnessing to followers of Eastern religions?

A3. Not only religious views, but also basic views on *reality* separate Christianity and Eastern religions.

Q4. Why would anyone believe Christianity over Eastern religions?

A4. If one believes that this world is *real*, and if one longs for meaning and hope based on reality, he will choose Christianity over an Eastern religion.

Chapter 10

Q1. What is the New Age Movement?

A1. The New Age Movement is a contemporary spiritual movement that focuses on the restoration of a mystical awareness of humanity's *godlike* potential and ultimate absorption into eternal oneness with the divine.

Q2. What differences does Christianity have with the New Age Movement?

A2. Christianity and the New Age Movement have very little fundamental *agreement*.

Q3. What obstacles interfere with Christians witnessing to followers of the New Age Movement?

A3. Not only religious views, but also basic views on *reality* separate Christianity and the New Age Movement.

Q4. Why would anyone believe Christianity over the New Age Movement?

A4. If one wants his faith to be grounded in *facts*, he will choose Christianity over the New Age Movement.

Chapter 11

Q1. Why would someone not believe in God?

A1. Some do not believe in God because they do *not* want to, and they interpret the evidence accordingly.

Q2. Why would someone want to believe in God?

A2. Some believe in God because they *want* to, and they interpret the evidence accordingly.

Q3. What is the great wager?

A3. The great wager we all make is in *staking* our lives on whether there is or is not a God.

Chapter 12

Q1. Why do we need to tell stories?

A1. We need to tell stories to accommodate how people *listen* and *learn*.

Q2. What story should we tell?

A2. We should tell our story of how we *accepted* God's story (the gospel).

Q3. How must we validate our story?

A3. We must validate our story with personal *integrity*.

ABOUT THE AUTHOR

Max Anders (Th.M. Dallas Theological Seminary, D.Min. Western Seminary) is the author of over twenty books and the creator and general editor of the thirty-two-volume Holman Bible Commentary. Dr. Anders has taught on the college and seminary level, was one of the original team members with Walk Thru the Bible Ministries, and has pastored for over twenty years. He is the founder and president of 7 Marks, Inc., a ministry specializing in discipleship strategies and materials for local churches (www.7marks.org). His book *30 Days to Understanding the Bible* has reached more than 300,000 readers with a passion for learning God's Word.

CPSIA information can be obtained
at www.ICGtesting.com
Printed in the USA
LVHW030009070723
751797LV00036B/1065

9 781401 675363